THE
COLONEL

THE
COLONEL

*The Captivating Biography of
the Dynamic Founder
of a Fast-food Empire*

John Ed Pearce

DOUBLEDAY & COMPANY, INC.
GARDEN CITY, NEW YORK   1982

Library of Congress Cataloging in Publication Data
Pearce, John Ed.
The Colonel.

1. Sanders, Harland, 1890–
2. Restaurateurs—Kentucky—Biography.
I. Title.
TX910.5.S25P4   338.7′6164795′0924 [B]
ISBN: 0-385-18122-1   AACR2

ISBN: 0-385-18122-1
Library of Congress Catalog Card Number 81-43856

Foreword

Colonel Harland Sanders was truly a unique man, not because he wore a white suit and a goatee, or because he became the symbol of an enormously successful product. He was a man of imagination, vision, and the courage to pursue that vision that changed the eating habits of the world.

His life is an inspiration. It is proof that the Great American Dream still exists, that if you have a better idea, the imagination to sell it, and the will to outwork the competition, it is still possible to achieve great things. His life should be a constant reminder to senior citizens that "the best is yet to be," for his rise to the heights did not even begin until after he reached retirement age. When members of the United States Congress asked what one should do to prepare for retirement, he responded, "Give him an opportunity to do for himself. NEVER STOP WORKING. A man will rust out before he wears out."

The legend of Colonel Sanders will always live in the state that he loved, and which he promoted around the world, personifying the state's reputation for warm hospitality as well as his own quality product. But I believe this book will prove that he was more than an image, a symbol. I will remember him as a brilliant man with a gourmet flair for food, a visionary and a great motivator, with the style of a showman and the discipline of a Vince Lombardi.

Those of us who were part of the Colonel's early family and franchisees will remember him as a creator, almost a father, the leader and teacher of a small group of business people who hung their hopes on the Colonel's dream and worked together to make that dream come true.

It has been said that you are fortunate if, in a lifetime, you can meet enough great people to count on one hand. In my lifetime I have had the opportunity to meet and know nine Presidents, most of the political and business leaders of our country, but the Colonel still stands as one of those great men you can count on one hand.

As Shakespeare wrote in *Hamlet*, "He was a man. Take him for all and all. We shall not look upon his like again."

John Young Brown, Jr.
Governor
Commonwealth of Kentucky

Prologue

With state police cruisers shepherding it through the early-morning traffic along Interstate 64, the hearse rolls along the Kentucky countryside between Shelbyville and the state capital of Frankfort, where eight state troopers, their breath white in the December chill, stand in facing rows at the eastern entrance of the looming gray capitol building. Silently they lift the dark casket from the hearse, carry it up the broad steps, through the bronze doors, and down the long marble corridor to the solemn, quiet rotunda where the statues of Kentucky's famed sons—Abraham Lincoln, Henry Clay, Jefferson Davis, Alben Barkley—regard the ages. As the troopers and their burden pass the doors of capitol offices, workers stand watching, murmuring to each other.

"He's here."

"Who?"

"The Colonel. They're bringing him in."

The troopers' footsteps echo softly around the towering marble walls of the rotunda as they place the casket on a bier, step back, and salute. A man from the Hall-Taylor Funeral Home in Shelbyville bustles about, placing the brass stanchions linked by velvet rope to form a corridor through which will pass those coming to view the body. Then he lifts the lid of the casket to reveal the familiar features, the white hair and goatee, the white suit and string tie, that marked Colonel Harland David Sanders, the man who parlayed a recipe for fried chicken into a business empire, launched the era of fast food, and became recognized around the world.

A few minutes later, Governor John Young Brown, Jr., handsome and graying in a dark-blue suit, strides through the southern entrance to the rotunda, flanked by aides, and drapes the blue-and-gold flag of the Commonwealth of Kentucky over the lid of the open casket. For a moment he stands there, looking down at the body of the man with whom his own life had been so intertwined, with whom he had joked and argued and built a vast fortune. Almost imperceptibly he shakes his head, as though finding it hard to believe that all of the tireless energy and restless drive that had marked the life of this man and had set him apart is gone. Then he walks quickly back to his office, the aide disappears down the hallway, and in a few minutes the first of the people who, for the next eight hours, will file past the casket come quietly, uncertainly into the rotunda.

Shortly after lunch, officials and politicians and state employees crowd into the space around the casket to hear Governor Brown eulogize the Colonel as "an American original, unique and uniquely American." He speaks not only of the famous man in the white suit, but of the man he has known through the years of business pull and haul, the man of temper and tenderness, of sudden rages and patient affection, the man who dreamed large dreams, and clung to hope when only hope was left. He quotes from *Hamlet*: "He was a man. Take him for all and all. We shall not look upon his like again."

Late in the afternoon, the body is returned to the Sanders home in Shelbyville, and the next morning is taken the twenty-five miles to Louisville. There, in the huge Southern mansion-style offices of Kentucky Fried Chicken, Inc., he again lies in state, a few feet from his old office and from the Colonel Sanders Museum, full of mementos of his career and tokens of the international empire he built on faith, hope, and sweat. Hundreds of company officials and friends, many of them wet-eyed, file past.

Again the casket is returned to the hearse, this time for a journey across town to the Southern Baptist Theological Seminary, where even the vast chapel cannot accommodate all those who have come to the funeral services, state and national politicians, leaders of business and industry, celebrities of sport and entertainment, old friends and business associates. Claudia Sanders, the Colonel's widow, weeps quietly but then smiles as the Reverend Ed Cayce tells of the Colonel's generosity, his temper, his humor, and his penchant for playing Cupid.

Then the final journey to a lot in Louisville's Cave Hill Cemetery, a lot he had chosen seven years earlier with instructions that, when she should die, Claudia should be brought here to lie beside him. A huge choir sings and the crowd pushes toward the grave site. There is some confusion as the line of cars and buses stretches beyond the winding roads of the cemetery out into the encircling streets, where people cannot find parking places.

Finally it is done. The family, the friends, the mourners, the curious, the attendants are gone. Dusk falls gently, and a cold wind blows across the fresh grave and the stone where the bust of the Colonel is backed by four marble pillars. It is quiet now, a curious note on which to end the life of a man who had known so little quiet, whose life had been so filled with movement and clashes and action. After roaming the world, Harland Sanders had come back to rest, only a few miles from where he had begun, just across the Ohio River, on a small farm outside Henryville, Indiana.

"You didn't get very far, did you?" the author of this book had once asked him jokingly.

"Far enough," Sanders replied with a chuckle. "About fifty miles."

Fifty miles. And ninety years. And two marriages, two daughters, and a son who died young. And lost jobs and automobile accidents, a gunfight and disappointments that made him sit, stomach-sick, with his head in his hands. And sweat and fever, cracked knuckles and seasickness, love and a split scalp and a stepfather's kicks. And work. Year after year of work. And hope, always hope. And the love of children, and the company of the powerful, and success of which few men dare to dream.

"Far enough," he said. "And always glad to get back."

And so he had, for the final time, come back.

THE
COLONEL

1

The house where he was born, on September 9, 1890, is no longer there. Old-timers in Henryville think that it burned down around the time of World War I. There is no trace of it now in the weedy field along the side road, three miles east of town, that leads past the Mount Moriah Church.

But it wasn't much of a house, anyhow, as Harland David Sanders remembered it—a thin-walled, four-room frame with a few steps leading to the front door and a back porch where his mother kept "stuff from the garden," and kindling wood and tools, a washtub and a scrubbing board. Not that he remembers the years there as particularly unpleasant, but the house, like his young years, offered few amenities. "Well, it was hard," he would recall. "I guess that's what you could say."

It would have been better if his father had lived. Wilbert Sanders was a mild, easygoing man who tried hard to make a go of his small farm. But he injured his back and leg in a fall, never recovered his strength, and was forced to take a job as a butcher in Henryville. Harland liked to visit his father in the butcher shop. Unlike most children, he loved liver, and would cry when his father pared off the bloody slices and wrapped them in the small white "boats" that butchers used, fearing that he would give it all away and leave none for the family. "I don't think Daddy made much money butchering," Harland said. "But we ate."

But there came a day, in 1895, when his father came home in the middle of the day and went to bed, and Harland's mother cautioned the children to be quiet, that their daddy wasn't feeling well. For a long time, his daddy had a fever. Twice the doctor came. And then one day Harland watched as his mother ran out of the house and down the road to their next-door neighbor's, and later the doctor came out from town and looked at his daddy and then talked to his mother in the kitchen. Harland remembered seeing his mother sitting at the kitchen table, crying, and that scared him, because he had never seen his mother cry before.

But she cried then, and hugged Harland and told him that his daddy had gone to be with God in heaven, and that now he was going to have to be her helper, and help her take care of Clarence, who was three, and Catherine, who was just a baby. At five, Harland was not old enough to appreciate his loss. But when they came and put his daddy in the coffin and took him out to be buried, Harland felt empty and frightened, and he sensed that everything was changing. He had heard his relatives and neighbors talking about who was going to take care of them. His mother, before her marriage, had been a Dunlevy, from down the road in New Albany, and now her people did what they could to help. There wasn't enough money for a fancy stone in the little cemetery across the road from the church. Years later, Harland would come back and replace the small marker with a dignified headstone bearing the names and years of his parents: WILBERT D. SANDERS, 1866–1895. MARGARET ANN SANDERS, 1865–1935.

From that day on, life in the Sanders household was pretty

much a matter of survival. While the children grew up with a
fondness for their mother and for each other, and with the
usual happy memories of childhood, life let them know in a
hurry that even childhood had its responsibilities.

Margaret Ann Sanders was a woman who believed in facing
life without whining. The descendant of Irish and Dutch set-
tlers who had come down the Ohio in the second quarter of
the nineteenth century, she had been reared in the philosophy
that work and Christian conduct were the keys to survival and
respect, and she determined to pass on these virtues to her
children. A portrait of her that hangs in the Sanders Museum
in Louisville is revealing. A stocky woman of medium height,
she possessed the physical strength and energy that her husband lacked, qualities her elder son obviously inherited from
her, just as he inherited the often conflicting qualities evident
in her face—the strong, rounded jaw, the tough chin in contrast to the rather tender mouth and humorous eyes, all fore-
telling Harland's blend of temper and tenderness, humor and
stubbornness.

But she faced a glum prospect. To be widowed and poor at
thirty with three small children was bad enough; to make matters worse, she lived in the country. For a while, she tried to
get by doing sewing and housework for neighbors, and by
letting the farm out on shares, so that she could stay home
while Harland went to school. But work was hard to find, just
as it was hard to find anyone to work such a small farm. When
Harland was seven, she took a job in the tomato-canning plant
in Henryville. Harland was left to take care of Clarence and
Catherine.

This was not too unusual. Children were often expected to
assume responsibility at a very young age. Older children were
expected to take care of the younger ones, and the younger
ones were expected to obey and learn from the older children
as well as from the parents. And it was not, apparently, an
unpleasant experience. Children adapt. At first, the three children were uneasy when their mother left early each morning,
but they soon came to take it as a fact of life: waving goodbye

in the morning, running down the road to meet her as she returned in the evening. And the days were spent in carefree play. They had the run of the house, and explored the fields and the woods beyond, picking flowers, shrilling at the occasional rabbit or snake that fled from their path, playing the games children find to play. There was no concern for security.

One thing that Harland learned at an early age was how to cook. He learned by watching his mother, and she taught him as much as time allowed, mainly because she had no choice; when she was away, there was no one else to do it. And sometimes, at the end of a long day in the canning plant, because she did not want to face the long walk home or because she longed for a few hours of social life, she would spend the night in town with friends or her cousin. That left Harland to see that the smaller children were fed, washed, and put to bed.

So Harland saw nothing unusual in his first experiment with baking. He had watched his mother and knew, generally, what to do.

"I ran Clarence and Catherine out of the kitchen," he recounted, "and set the yeast, like she'd done. Then I made the sponge, and mixed it and let it rise, got the oven hot, and put in the loaf. I kept watching it, and when I figured it was done, I took it out and let it cool. Then I gave Catherine and Clarence some. Well, they thought it was good. They said it was so good we ought to show it to Mama. So we took off down the road, carrying the bread, and me and Clarence almost carrying Catherine, and the dust on the road so thick it squirted up between our toes—we went barefoot in the summer, don't you see. We must have been a sight when we walked into the canning plant and looked around for Mama to show her the bread."

The bread was a great success. All of the women on the canning line had to try a bite, and all felt called upon to give the fledgling baker a hug or kiss. "I hated that," Harland said later. "You know how little boys are; hate to be messed with like that."

But too much affection was not to be a major problem for

young Harland. His mother was not a demonstrative woman, and there was no one else to show him affection. In the winter, he went to school, but he was not good in school, and not very happy, never mixing too well with the children from town and considering himself something of an outsider. In the summer, he took care of the children so that his mother could work in town and save a little money against the winter. Just how much schooling Harland had is uncertain. In his later years, he claimed to have dropped out of school in the sixth grade because he became irritated with the insubstantial theories of algebra, but the fact seems to be that he lacked incentive and encouragement. He did not lack intelligence. Later, he was able to teach himself a smattering of law, and he was good with figures, though the intricacies of corporate finance puzzled and bored him. But there is no doubt that his lack of education handicapped him, especially in his own mind. Throughout his life, he was self-conscious about his lack of polish and his habitual use of coarse language, which he attributed to his inability to express himself.

He had become accustomed to taking care of Clarence and Catherine and helping his mother around the house when, in the summer of his tenth year, his life suddenly changed. The day after school had let out for the summer, his mother called him into the kitchen and told him that she had found a job for him.

"Mr. Charlie Norris, lives over the other side of Henryville, says he'll give you your keep and two dollars a month for helping him on his farm," she said. "It'll be good for you. You'll learn things that'll help you, and you'll get a chance to earn some money. You think you can do it?"

"Sure," he said, and the sight of him standing there, only a child and full of a child's uncertainty, but trying to act big and tough, touched his mother's heart, and she pulled him to her in a sudden and rare embrace.

"You'll do fine," she assured him.

Harland wasn't too sure. He was a little excited at the idea of seeing new places and making some real money. But he was scared, too, at the thought of being away from home. The next morning his mother put his clothes in a paper bag and walked with him the few miles down the road, through Henryville and on to the Norris farm.

Charlie Norris was a large, serious, no-nonsense man who lived by the hard demands of a small Indiana farm.

"This him?" he asked when Margaret Ann presented Harland at the back door of the big unpainted frame house.

"This is Harland," she replied, shoving him forward gently.

"Well, he looks sturdy enough," said Norris, not smiling, but not unkindly.

"He's a good boy," said his mother, "and a good worker." After a few moments in which nothing was said, she turned to go. Harland watched her walk down the road, leaving him to his first job.

"Well, come on, boy," said Norris, who was not a man to waste time or words, and Harland followed him into the house, where he met Mrs. Norris, who was equally sparing of conversation, and was shown the small room where he would sleep. There was little in it other than a bed, but he would have no use for more. His days were to be spent working.

Workdays on the Norris farm started early and ended late. Harland was up before daybreak to help Norris with the chores in the barn, and after a silent breakfast began his job clearing brush and scrubwood from land adjoining the planted fields. It was not particularly hard work, but the woods were full of birds and squirrels, rabbits scurried in and out of the fencerow brambles, and there were wild flowers among the weeds. There was no one to keep him to his task, and he took to spending a lot of time lying on his back looking and listening to the sounds of nature. By the end of the month, he had cleared very little land, and Charlie Norris was not a man to pay a boy good money to listen to the birds.

"Is this all you've got done?" he demanded when he came out to see how his new farmhand was progressing. "Come on to the house."

In the kitchen, he said simply, "Get your stuff." After Harland had put his meager belongings into his paper bag, he went back to the kitchen, wordlessly waiting for the verdict.

"Here's the two dollars I told your ma I'd pay you," said Norris. "Now get on home. You're not worth a daggone, boy."

It was a painful walk home. Harland hung around outside the house for a long time, dreading the prospect of facing his mother.

"What are you doing home, son?" she asked him when he finally slunk into the house.

"Mr. Norris let me go," he said, not looking at her.

"Why'd he do that, son?"

Harland squirmed, but gradually told his story.

"Sit down, son," his mother said, and in the next few minutes gave Harland a tongue-lashing that he said he never forgot.

"It looks like you'll never amount to anything," she said calmly. "I'm afraid you're just no good. Here I am, left alone with you three children to support, and you're my oldest boy, the only one that can help me, and you won't even work enough so somebody will keep you. I guess I'll never be able to count on you."

(Eighty years later, Harland's second wife would say, "I think that talking-to by his mother was one of the things that drove him in life. He wanted so much to prove she was wrong when she said he was no good, and it got him into the habit of driving hard.")

"I felt bad about it," Harland admitted later. "Felt bad for her. I'd let her down, don't you see, and I knew it; and I said then and there that if I ever got another job, I'd do it right. And after that, I never got fired from another job." (That wasn't true, as a matter of fact, but he never again was fired for being lazy. The next summer, when he got another farm job, he swore he would do better, and did.)

This job was with Henry Monk, who worked a bigger farm down in the southern part of the county, near New Albany. Monk was a kind man, but he had agreed to pay Harland four dollars a month and keep, and for this he expected work, with little allowance for the fact that his new hand was only eleven. On the first morning, he hitched three teams to plows and handed the reins of one team to Harland.

"Here, boy," he said, "this here is yours," and headed the lead team down the long field, followed by his other hired hand, a tall, lanky eighteen-year-old. Harland grabbed the reins and struggled to follow. It was a long morning.

At noon they walked back to the house, ate silently, and as silently returned to the field. By dusk, Harland was wobbling and glassy-eyed with fatigue, only to find that after supper he was required to join Monk in the barn, feeding, watering, and milking the cows. He was not a good milker, and twice the cow kicked him, almost overturning the milk pail. Harland claimed later that Monk always gave him the sore-teated cows, and it took him a while to learn to evade the kicks. And by the time he finally reached his upstairs room, he was too tired to take off his clothes before falling onto the hard bed. The next morning he was so sore he could hardly move.

So the days went: up before the sun, seldom finished with the chores before ten at night. Life, it seemed to him, was the sight of the rear end of a horse or the feel of the warm side of a cow, and the tug of a plow that wanted to wobble from side to side or that threatened to flip him against the horse when it hit a rock.

But he stuck. His hands blistered and toughened; the muscles in his arms and shoulders thickened from the strain of holding the plow to a furrow. He began to feel a glow of pride when he caught Monk regarding him with a half-smile or heard his tone of approval. He was almost sorry to see the summer end.

"You did all right, boy," Monk said as he handed him his wages. "Did all right. You want a job next summer, I'll see if I can't find something for you."

Harland returned home with a new sense of dignity, and more money than he had ever had. But he had learned now what it was like to be on his own, to do a man's work, make a living. After that, school seemed childish and a waste of time. More than ever, he felt different from the other children. He was ready to quit.

His mother did little to encourage him, probably because she was so weary from holding the family together that she had little time or energy to listen or help. Clarence and Catherine were getting bigger, and more money was needed for their school, clothes, and food. Sickness serious enough to bring the doctor was a crisis, if only because of the expense. When Harland was twelve, she called him in and asked him to sit down at the table.

"You know Mr. Broaddus that's been stopping by to see us?" she asked. Harland nodded.

"Well," she said, "he's asked me to marry him, and I've said I would."

Her words hit him like a slap across the face. He had been aware that the tall, heavyset Broaddus had been dropping around more and more often, and he had felt a vague sense of uneasiness at the way his mother and the strange man sat and talked. He was too young to appreciate that his mother was a lonely and tired young woman, uneasy about the future. He could think only of how his home was being threatened with change. Someone he didn't even know was intruding on their tight circle. His position as the man of the house was in jeopardy. He stared at his mother with hurt and indignation.

"He's got a place up in Greenwood where we can live," she continued, looking at him tenderly, hoping he could understand the forces pressing in upon her. "He's promised to take good care of all of us. And you know how hard it's been with us lately."

"Yeah," he said finally. "I guess so."

A few days later, Margaret Ann and Mr. Broaddus went off toward Henryville together, and when they came back they called the children in and told them that they were married.

The months that followed were not happy ones for Harland, and it is likely that the marriage proved to be no easy bargain for Margaret Ann. William Broaddus had wanted a wife.

There is no evidence that he wanted the children she brought with her, and his attitude toward the gangling, independent, often resentful Harland was not that of a loving father. Broaddus was a hard man. He expected life to be hard, and he had no patience with anyone who did not regard it grimly. There was no humor, laughter, or levity in his life. He worked.

Broaddus was a truck gardener, cultivating a small farm near Greenwood, Indiana, and selling his produce at the market in Indianapolis. He saw to it that Harland did his share of the work.

"Fridays, we'd get up at midnight," Harland recalled, "and drive into Indianapolis and set up at the marketplace around the courthouse. We had to get the stalls set up by three in the morning, so that the grocers could get their stuff fresh for the morning trade, don't you see? It didn't take long to sell out, and then we'd head back home for a day's work. I didn't care for getting up that early. I had a hard time staying awake after we got set up and were waiting for the grocers to get what they wanted. Then I'd be sleepy all day. He didn't like that. He didn't like much of anything I did.

"I worked like a Trojan for that man, but it didn't do. He had money, and at first he talked about how he would take care of us and all, but stepchildren just didn't fit in. It just wasn't there for him to have any use for us. I forget what it was that made him mad, but one day he just kicked me all over the kitchen. I dodged around until I got by the door, and then I lit out for the barn. I stayed there till dark, and then slipped back in and got my clothes, then went back and spent the night in the barn. I'd made up my mind to leave."

Torn between husband and son, and the need for holding the family together, his mother decided it would be best if Harland left. It couldn't have been an easy decision. For all his outward toughness, and the fact that she had been able to depend on him for years, Harland was still only a twelve-year-old boy. But things couldn't go on as they were. The next morning, when Broaddus left the house, she brought out her battered paper suitcase and together they packed his meager belongings.

"You go down to your Uncle Dick's," she told him. "You know where he lives. We've been there. Tell him I sent you. He'll help you."

It was a painful departure for young Harland. He bid goodbye to Mother and Catherine. Clarence, trying not to cry and not knowing what to say, walked with him down to the road and forlornly said goodbye. Harland walked until he was out of sight, and then sat down and cried. Then he got up, wiped his eyes on his sleeve, and started walking toward New Albany. A man came by in a wagon, heading for "the state line," which meant the Ohio River, and Harland rode along with him. Late in the day, he found the home of his uncle, Dick Dunlevy, who welcomed him, listened to his story, and put him in an upstairs room with the rest of the children. He felt a surge of homesickness, not for Greenwood, but for their old home back in Henryville, as he fell asleep. But in the morning, it was all behind him. He sensed that his childhood had ended, and that a new life was about to begin. Two days later Clarence turned up, having also decided to leave home rather than endure the unhappiness that had invaded it. But by that time, Harland had moved on. With his uncle's help, he had found a job. He was on his own.

2

Harland nearly always had a job. This was no special credit to him; he had no choice. There were no welfare laws to help families with dependent children. Neither were there any child labor laws to keep a healthy boy from working. With his uncle's help, Harland got a job working on a farm, and within a year he was regarded as a full-fledged hand. He could hitch a team, plow, milk, stretch fence, weed, hay, lay by crops, clean the barn, chop wood, and do the rudimentary carpentry necessary to keep a farm going. Before he quit, when he was fourteen, he was making two dollars a week and keep, enough to let him go into New Albany on Sunday afternoons and hang around.

He found the trips to town both exciting and disturbing. He liked to watch the boats on the river, mingle with the people walking along the wharf, gaze into the store windows, and see the big homes. But watching the other young people gave him a feeling of inadequacy, of being gawky and different. He felt country and awkward in his overalls. He felt the town kids were snickering at him, boys who, he knew, couldn't stand up to a plow, never made a penny in their lives, didn't know half the stuff he did. He resented them, yet he wanted to be more like them.

He found relief from these disquieting emotions by watching the trains. He could watch them by the hour: the black smoke pouring from the stack, the coughing rhythm as the big drivers churned on the rails, the haughty grandeur of the engineer as he leaned out the window of the cab, the adventure that seemed to ride with the men in the caboose. He felt for the first time an urge, a longing, to go somewhere, to see the world.

He was tired of farming, tired of the backbreaking work that seemed always to get done just in time to be done again, and tired of the low pay. Compared with what he saw people in town doing, the chores of the farm seemed dull and monotonous. He was more than ready to try something new when his Uncle Dick came to his rescue. Dick Dunlevy, a hearty, jovial, hardworking Irishman, worked for the New Albany Street Car Company, and when the company announced that it was looking for a fare collector, he suggested that Harland apply. Harland did, wearing a suit that one of his cousins lent him, and got the job. It wasn't, he decided at once, a bad job. He had a blue uniform, complete with a billed cap, and his duties consisted chiefly of walking along the aisle between the rows of cane-bottomed seats and collecting fares.

"Fares," he would call. "Fares, please." He liked New Albany, with its streets leading down to the river and the clanging of the streetcar bell. He learned to make change rapidly, and got to know the customers who rode the car regularly. Between stops he chatted with some of them, another feature of the job that he liked. He might have stayed with the streetcar company indefinitely had it not been for one of the regulars, a man who worked at the U. S. Army Quartermaster Depot.

"One day this fellow motioned to me," Harland recalled,

"and said, 'Boy, Uncle Sam is looking for young fellows to
volunteer for a hitch in Cuba with the Army.' That was during
the time after the Platt Amendment was passed, giving us the
right to intervene in Cuba if there was any trouble with them
holding elections. And they were having trouble as usual, so it
seemed, so we were sending troops down to help keep order
during the election. Anyhow, this fellow said it ought to be a
lot of adventure for a young man, a chance to see some of the
world, get out of New Albany, and said I ought to think about
it.

"Well, I thought about it, and I thought, well, I was getting
on, and it was maybe time I saw something of the world, did
something different, so next day I went down to Jeffersonville
and told them I wanted to sign up. I told them I was twenty-
one. [He was actually not yet sixteen.] I guess I ought to be
ashamed of lying, but in those days you weren't blamed too
much for a little lie if you needed it to get a job. Lots of boys
lied about their age or about what they could do, and took a
chance on being able to do it when they got the job. Which I
think was all right. There's no trick to doing a job when you
already know how. It's being able to catch on quick and hold it
when you don't know nothing except how to sweat; that's
when you earn it. Anyhow, they didn't ask me nothing, just
told me to sign, and I did, and the next day they put me and
four other fellows on a train for Norfolk."

He liked the train ride, but there was where the liking
stopped. Four days later, he shipped out for Cuba, on what he
later described as "the most miserable thing any man ever
went through." He had never seen a body of water bigger than
the Ohio River, or a boat bigger than the steamers around the
Louisville wharves. Before he was out of sight of land, the
slow, incessant surge and roll of the ship made him hopelessly
seasick. Aside from the few soldiers aboard, the only cargo was
fifteen hundred mules, and Harland was one of those assigned
to care for them. The stench of manure and mules added to
the nausea induced by the ship's cruel motion. Harland

weighed a strapping 168 pounds when he left Norfolk. He weighed a wretched 127 when they finally docked in Havana Harbor.

"I was as sick as a man could get and live," he remembered. "I never could ride the water after that."

The Cuban elections went off without serious incident and, with the crisis past, the new soldiers were allowed to sign out of the Army and go home if they wanted to.

"And I wanted to," said Harland. "I was so homesick I figured getting home was even worth a ride with the mules. So I said I wanted out, and in a couple of months us that wanted out were shipped back. I wasn't as sick on the way home, but I never wanted any more of the ocean. I remember how good New Orleans looked when we got in there."

When the ship docked in New Orleans, he took leave of the Army and, with no job but a little money in his pocket, he decided to bum around for a while and see the country. He caught a freight train up the river and spent a few days in St. Louis. Assured that he wouldn't get seasick on the river, he got a job as a deckhand on a riverboat down to Memphis. Then for a summer he hopped freight trains around the South, feeling free and adventurous, dropping off in strange towns and sometimes finding a few days' work so that he wouldn't run completely out of eating money. He loved the trains, loved the smell of the coal smoke and the steam streaming back past the cars, loved the clack of the wheels, the lean of the cars on curves, the wailing warning of the whistle. He loved to stand by a water tank and watch the fireman grab the chain and pull down the big spout, sending the water for the boilers gushing into the tender.

One day he dropped off a freight in Sheffield, Alabama, and remembered that his Aunt Kate, his mother's sister, and his Uncle John lived there. Before leaving New Albany for his nauseating hitch in the Army, he had visited his mother, and remembered that she had told him that Clarence was staying with Kate. He was eager to see "some of my own," and he re-

membered his mother saying that Uncle John worked for the
Southern Railroad. It occurred to him that maybe Uncle John
could help him get a job with the railroad.

At his uncle's home, he enjoyed a reunion with Clarence,
who was fourteen now and working at a feed store, and who
filled him in on news of the family. His mother was still married to Broaddus; Catherine was growing up and looked like
their mother. For the first time in months, Harland wrote
home. He enjoyed his visit, and when his uncle offered to help
him find work with the railroad, his heart leaped. He could see
himself sitting in the cab of a locomotive, looking tough in his
cap and goggles, leaning out the window to watch the tracks.
It was not to be so glamorous.

"I got a job in the roundhouse as a blacksmith's helper. I'd as
soon been back farming. That blacksmith was a mean man.
Always pushing us, forcing us to hammer the iron before it was
hot enough, and let me tell you, that was no easy job. But I
said I wouldn't quit, and I didn't."

Long months followed, months of cold steel and a bitter
boss, and a boy playing the role of a man, with blistered hands
and cracked knuckles, and helpers muttering that hell would
be full of blacksmiths working cold iron. Harland stayed for a
while at his uncle's home, but there wasn't much room and
soon he moved into a boardinghouse near the railroad yards,
and began to spend some of his time off around the town
movie house and a nearby poolroom. And for the first time, he
began to take an interest in girls.

"I was like any other young buck, I guess," he remembered.
"I just never had any chance, any time, to get used to them,
and I was a little bashful. Nervous, don't you see? I guess that
was the first time, too, that I learned to watch my talk. I hadn't
had much school, you see, and didn't know how to talk much,
talk right, and I'd been picking up a lot of cussin', I guess to
make me sound older, sound tough. So I had to watch myself
when the girls came by and we would try to get them to walk
with us. That's what we did. We'd say hello to a girl, and if she

said hello back, we'd just fall in step with them and walk around the downtown with them, or maybe, if we was doing all right, walk them home."

Harland's career as the budding great lover of Sheffield was cut short, however, when he heard through the railroad grapevine that there was a job as a yard worker in Jasper. He caught a Southern freight up to Jasper and put in his bid. It wasn't a big promotion, but it was better than his job as a blacksmith's helper. He cleaned out the ashpans of the locomotives and filled the sandboxes that released the gritty sand onto the tracks to give the big driver wheels traction. He began to think that he was going to spend the rest of his life shaking out fireboxes and carrying pails of sand, when one morning he heard one of the stationmen telling the engineer of a locomotive that his fireman was sick, and that there was no backup fireman handy. Harland had never fired before, but he knew a little about the job from having watched firemen at work and from hearing them talk about their job as they slouched at the lunch counter where crews rested over coffee and sandwiches at the end of their runs. He walked to the cab and looked up at the man in the goggles.

"Mister," he said to the engineer, "I can fire that engine."

"You ever fired, son?"

"No," he answered, "but I can try, and you ain't got nobody else."

The engineer laughed.

"Well, you look stout enough," he said. "If you think you can do it, we'll give her a try."

All day the would-be fireman worked and sweated, battling to satisfy the hungry flames of the firebox, trying to keep up the pressure on the steam gauge, fighting for balance on the swaying platform of the locomotive, learning how to ram the scoop under the coal, to lift with his legs, to swing the scoop with his body and not his arms, to turn and swing with one motion, and to time his swing so that the coal went squarely into the box, keeping the floor of the cab clean. It had seemed

easy when he saw other men do it; it was not easy now. But at
the end of the run, the engineer looked at him and said, "You
didn't do bad." It was a high moment, in spite of his throbbing
back and trembling thighs. The next morning the trainmaster
called him into the office. The engineer, he said, had given him
a good report.

"You want to try to be a fireman?" the trainmaster asked.
Harland admitted he'd like to try.

"Well, there's your run," the man said, nodding toward an
engine down the track. "Hop to it."

Harland grabbed his cap and gloves and walked down the
yard, swaggering past the lowly hand filling sandboxes. He
swung into the cab. A fireman. He was not quite seventeen.
But he was almost grown, heavyset and strong, almost six feet
tall and weighing 185 pounds, and he liked the hard work. And
he bulged with pride at being a professional, a bona fide
member of a train crew, along with the engineer, conductor,
and brakeman.

At first, he got a short run, Jasper to Paris. Then came the
big hauls, the long runs down to Mobile, up into Tennessee,
roaring through the pine woods, rumbling across the black
trestles high above clay-red rivers, whistling through the towns
where the stations flashed by and little boys stood beside the
track to wave. Leaning into the shovel, taking a measured step,
swinging in rhythm to the sway of the train, feeding the firebox, kicking the door closed, feeling the fire on his face and the
sweat down his shirt. Easing to stop at the water tank, listening to the slosh of the water, pushing up the spout, then leaning again into the shovel as the stack coughed in quickening
bursts and tugged the train to life. Inhaling the fragrant mixture of steam and coal smoke, watching as night fell and the
whistle howled through the darkness and oases of light blurred
past and the firebox door swung open and the glare lit up the
face of the engineer as he checked his gauges and opened the
throttle.

He was a real railroad man now, good at his job, learning
the instruments and gauges of the cab, learning the signals of

train and track by which the engineer guided his haul, learning
to relax when the engineer eased the train onto a siding, glory-
ing in the dust that blackened his overalls by the end of a long
run, learning to wear his bandanna loose around his throat so
that he could wipe the sweat and dust from his eyes. He liked
the night runs, liked to see dawn break over the sleeping countryside as they tore through the little towns, liked to sit at the
counters of the dimly lit stations, savoring the smell of coal
smoke and cooking food, swapping talk with the other railroad
men, growing to manhood, doing a man's work.

For almost three years, he worked as a fireman for Southern
Railroad, confident now that the day would come when he
would run his own train. But when he took off his gloves, it
was not to step up to the engineer's job. In later life, he always
insisted that after he was fired from that first job on Charlie
Norris' farm, he never lost another job. But he did now. He
was fired.

The year was 1910. Harland was twenty. The wild days of
railroading were coming to an end. Train crews had a union
now, the Brotherhood of Locomotive Firemen and Engineer-
men, and Harland, as soon as he joined, became active in
union affairs. Not that he was any great union man or harbored any resentment against management. Throughout his
life, he would be a joiner, using the organization he joined to
promote himself more than any cause. In the union, he got to
be a member of the grievance committee, listening to the complaints of members and taking them to the regional office
when action seemed justified. A case came before the committee in which a man had been fired through what was clearly a
mistake—another man of the same name had broken a safety
rule. Harland pleaded the case before the company board and
got the man restored to his job with a year's back pay. He felt
cocky about his success, but his engineer warned him that he
had made a mistake.

"You don't cost the line a year's pay without the bosses
remembering it," he told Harland. "Watch your step now. You
make a slip and they'll have your job."

A few weeks later, the glum prophecy came true. While on the run from Sheffield to Jasper, Harland became sick at his stomach. Having seen a fireman he knew get on a coach of the train at the station just past, Harland went back and asked the man to fire for him until he could recover. The man said sure, and Harland went into the baggage coach to lie down. As they pulled into the next station, Harland felt well enough to go back to work, and was just climbing over the tender as they pulled to a stop. As they did, he saw the trainmaster watching him.

"What're you doing back in the train, Sanders?" he called.

"Got sick," Harland told him. "Got my buddy to fire for me for a minute so I could lie down."

The next Monday he got notice he had been fired for insubordination. His appeal went nowhere.

"I came down out of that cab making seven dollars a day and went to work as a section hand making seventy cents a day," he said later, not without bitterness. "They didn't care if I worked at that because there was no union for section hands. That caused me bad trouble, and not just the money." The trouble stemmed from the fact that, not too long before, he had gotten married.

"I was down in Jasper," he recalled. "Went to a picture show with some other young people I'd met, and after the show we stood around outside, and I noticed this girl, named Josephine King. Caught her looking at me, or so I thought, and it turned out I was right, and I thought to myself she was a good-looker. So I went up and started talking to her, and pretty soon we left the rest of them and started walking, and I walked her home. After that we started seeing each other, don't you see, and after a few weeks it just seemed to me that she was looking forward to me coming to Jasper, and I was looking forward to seeing her, and it just seemed like time to get married. So we did. Married in a Christian church in Jasper, and moved into a place we rented up in Tuscumbia, about eighty miles from Jasper, where my run ended."

Josephine was a quiet, moody woman, two years older than Harland, and close to her large Alabama family. From the beginning, their marriage was often strained, and Harland complained of Josephine's unresponsiveness. She did not feel well during her first pregnancy, and Harland worried about her when he was away on his runs. They soon had a daughter, named Margaret, for his mother. The next year a son was born, Harland Jr. By that time, Harland had been fired by the Southern Railroad and his marriage was in trouble.

"Well, I was looking around for a job, of course, and I finally got one, firing for the Norfolk and Western. The trouble was that the N&W didn't run to Alabama and the job took me away from home all the time, and there we was with two babies. Well, after a while I was writing letters to my wife and not hearing from her, and naturally that worried me, especially with the babies so young. I liked the N&W all right, but I was worried. Then I got a letter from my brother-in-law saying that Josephine had gone back to her folks in Jasper. He said she never had no business marrying a no-good who couldn't hold a job, anyhow. And all the time I'd been sending home what I could."

Harland hotfooted it back to Tuscumbia, only to find that Josephine had, indeed, gone home. Not only had she left, but she had given up their home and given their furniture to their neighbors.

"That hurt me," he said. "I figured she didn't have any right to take my children and give away my furniture. But I didn't know anything to do about it."

As the days passed, he longed to see his children. Then, as so many fathers have done in similar circumstances, he devised a plan to kidnap them, "Although I didn't consider it rightly kidnapping, since they was mine." He decided that he would hang out in a small woods near his father-in-law's home, and when the children came out to play, he would grab them and head for the railroad station. Early one morning, he sneaked into the woods and lay down in the weeds to wait. He saw his

father-in-law leave, saw his mother-in-law come out on the
porch and go back in. He could hear voices from the house.
But the children didn't come out. The sun began to beat down
on him with an Alabama fierceness. His father-in-law returned.
A wagon drove by. He began to sweat, and flies buzzed
around him. A dog came by, growling and circling around
him, suspicious. Finally, feeling a little foolish, he concluded
that his plan wasn't going to work. But he couldn't just give up
and walk away. So, feeling conspicuous and trying not to seem
embarrassed, he stood up and walked across the field to the
house. Josephine's father was rocking on the porch.

"Howdy, Harland," he said without slowing his rocking or
changing expression, as if it was perfectly natural for Harland
to come walking in from the woods. "What are you doing in
town?"

"I came to see my family," Harland replied.

For a moment they eyed each other, and then the older man
said, "Well, sit down." They tried to make small talk for a
while, and then Harland stood up without explanation and
walked inside, where the children were playing on the floor
and Josephine was sitting on the sofa, as though expecting
him. They exchanged rather meaningless pleasantries, never
getting around to the reason why he was there, and after a
while, not knowing what else to do, he got up to leave.

"Where are you going?" Josephine asked.

"I've got a new job," he told her. "Going to work for the
Illinois Central."

"No," she said, not looking at him. "I think you better stay
with me."

And so he stayed with her, though not in Jasper. He stayed
with her for thirty-seven years. But looking back on the episode during the later years of his life, he admitted that, after
that, "Things were never the same between us, don't you see?"

Work on the railroad didn't turn out well, either. He became a fireman again with the Illinois Central, and was finally
given the privileged job of firing the crack Seminole Limited,

with a group of the railroad's top officials on board. They got off to a late start, but by leaning into the shovel, Harland got them into Haleyville on time.

"Boy," said the engineer, after they were in the station, "you sure know how to fire an engine."

Unfortunately, the trainmaster at the station was the same one who had gotten Harland fired for insubordination when he was working on the Southern. He reported Harland again, and the district supervisor called him in.

"Why didn't you tell me you were fired from the Southern for insubordination?" he demanded. "You know I'm going to have to let you go."

"You can't," snapped Harland. "Brotherhood rules say you can't have a blacklist. You let me go and I'll get a lawyer."

He got to keep his job, but not for long. One day in Jackson, Tennessee, Harland and his engineer got into an argument over some Brotherhood matters while they were waiting at the water tower by the roundhouse. Words led to curses, curses to blows, and soon they were rolling on the ground, mauling each other. The engineer demanded an investigation, which could have only one outcome. Harland was clearly guilty of insubordination, fighting on the job, and striking his engineer. He didn't wait to hear the verdict. He had heard that there was a fireman's job open on the Rock Island Line, and the next day he left for Little Rock to apply for it. He got the job but, again, didn't keep it long. His life was about to take a different turn. He was approaching twenty-five, but at a time when he should have been settling down to a life's work, he was starting on an era of hopping from one job to another, an unsettled and, in ways, an unsettling time.

He had been on his own for more than a decade, and the years were doing something to Harland Sanders. In his later years, he would insist that "I never did like to fight. I fought to get justice. A fellow has to stand up for himself. I never did like to get pushed around." The statement is revealing. True to his Irish blood and red hair, Harland had a temper, and he was not controlling it. A curious mixture of self-confidence, brashness, defensiveness, and feelings of inferiority, he often felt that life had not rewarded him sufficiently for his years of hard work, and resented the fact that other men did not seem to respect him. He was frustrated in his desire to get ahead, amount to something, and this conflict of emotions often led him to act and talk before he thought, and to react defensively when this got him into trouble. And it was to get him into trouble frequently.

3

"The Rock Island Line," according to folk song, "is a mighty fine line." It didn't prove so fine for Harland Sanders. When he got to Little Rock, he found that the fireman's job had been filled, and that the only thing open was a job as a lowly section hand. He took it. He had meant to send for Josephine and the children, but now he couldn't. They went home to stay with her parents in Jasper. Another daughter, Mildred, was born soon afterward.

Life as a section hand was no bed of roses. The work was hard. Harland had to live in a section car—a converted boxcar parked on a siding. Actually, he did not mind too much, because he had already decided that his future did not lie in railroading. The glamour world of his youth had lost much of its luster. He had decided that the law was his ticket to fame and fortune, and while he was working for the Illinois Central had begun taking correspondence courses in law. Now his nights were devoted to the books that would open the new world of opportunity to him.

At first, the lessons were baffling and frustrating. He felt again the handicap of his scanty education. But he had already become something of a reader, and he was too proud and too stubborn to give up and admit that he couldn't do it. On his off-hours, he visited local lawyers, who were sympathetic with his groping efforts, and were glad to interpret and explain the meaning of the legal terms. He began to see that the strange Latin words really did have meaning, that the law fell into a certain pattern.

There was logic in his choice of the law. In his work with the Brotherhood, he had found that success lay with the man who could understand and interpret the rules and argue convincingly for his interpretation of them, mixing appeals for justice and common sense with references to the rules. Furthermore, he was discovering in himself a talent that he would someday develop and utilize—a talent for acting. Harland Sanders was a performer. He had the ability to portray a character, and to feel, to become, what he was trying to project. And he loved the attention. He loved the limelight.

His opportunity to put his newfound knowledge to work came sooner than he expected. After a few weeks as a section hand, he had gotten back his old job of fireman, working on a passenger run from Brinkley to Newport, Arkansas. Each day his train had to pull off on a siding to let the Hot Springs Limited roar past. One day it was late, and the waiting crew finally heard that it had derailed a few miles down the line. A number of passengers had been injured.

Harland knew that, when such accidents occurred, it was railroad practice to get a claims adjuster to the scene as quickly as possible. This claims adjuster would try to get the injured passengers to sign statements releasing the railroad from liability, promising them in return as little as possible in the way of payment. Harland got an idea, born of his nights with the lawbooks. Racing to his room, he changed into his only suit, grabbed a handful of power-of-attorney forms, and hurried to the station where the accident victims had been taken. Talking fast, selling hard, he persuaded an injured passenger to give him the authority to represent him, convincing the passenger that he could get him a better settlement than the claims adjuster would offer. The man signed, and others, who had overheard, followed suit. While he was signing, the claims adjuster arrived and, seeing what was going on, began working the other side of the waiting room. They met and glared at each other, but Harland had a clear lead. He realized that his days with the railroad were over, but that made no difference. He was about to launch his new career.

The fact that he had no real credentials was not really important, since the law in those days permitted almost anyone with a smattering of legal knowledge to appear before the bar. A man "read the law" in some attorney's office until he felt competent to argue a case; he appeared before the bar as soon as he could find a client willing to hire him. Armed with his power-of-attorney forms and his smattering of legal terminology, Harland barged into court to represent his first clients. He did well, too. Not only did he win some substantial awards for his clients, but he earned about $2,500 in fees. The fact that he had received his notice of dismissal from the railroad was brushed aside. He was riding high.

With his new wealth—and $2,500 was a considerable amount of money in 1915—he rented a small house in Little Rock and sent for Josephine and the children. He then called on Judge Fred Isagrave, whose brother he had met in Jasper, and was given permission to use the judge's law library. He waded into the lawbooks with inspired energy, and was soon practicing before the local justice of the peace. Had he stuck with it, instead of getting sidetracked, there is every indication that Harland would have made a first-class trial lawyer.

But it was inevitable that Harland's life would be beset by problems. One of them was his brother Clarence, who had begun drinking. Clarence, who was now working for the Rock Island Line, had inherited his father's easygoing nature, as well as a weakness for alcohol. And, like many sons of funda-

mentalist, teetotaling families, he could not drink moderately.
One drink and he dived into the bottle, and Harland had little
success getting him out. Josephine became weary of having
Clarence brought reeling into the house for another dry-out
session. And often Harland had to spend time with him that he
could have spent more profitably preparing his legal cases. But
he had a strong sense of family, and he worried about Clarence. The country was about to be drawn into World War I,
and though Harland himself was exempt from conscription
because of his wife and children, Clarence was eligible, and
Harland worried over what might happen to him if conscription sent him to fight in Europe.

Even without the problem of Clarence, Harland's can-
tankerous nature soon embroiled him in what turned out to be
a losing cause. The decisions of the justices of the peace in
Arkansas were erratic, varying wildly from case to case. This
not only violated Harland's sense of justice, but threatened his
purse, since he had reason to suspect that he had lost some
cases, and some fees, because he was not splitting fees with the
justice of the peace involved. The situation had aroused an
effort among local attorneys to pass a law curbing the powers
of these corrupt dispensers of justice, and Harland jumped
headlong into the fray. Not content to be one of the battlers,
he became a vocal leader of the crusade, and at one point
appeared before a legislative committee at the state capital
and delivered an emotional plea for reform. He showed,
among other things, how a client of his had been forced by a
justice of the peace to pay a loan shark more than three hundred percent interest, only to have his wages garnisheed by the
same justice of the peace when he failed to make a final payment.

Harland was successful, to a degree. A law curbing some of
the powers of the JPs was passed, but he now found himself
thrown into the pit with the lions whose claws he had tried to
trim. And this handicap was compounded by his own tendency
toward self-destruction. Back at work in court in Little Rock,

he won damages for a client, but when the client demanded the check for his damages, Harland refused to hand it over until the client paid him his fee. It was a matter that should have been handled in the privacy of his office; instead, he allowed the argument to erupt in the courtroom in sight of the JP and other court officers.

Perhaps his stand was justified, but his remarks to the client were intemperate, and before the astonished eyes of the court, Attorney Sanders and his client began trading punches. Throughout his life, Harland insisted that he merely defended himself against the client, who attacked him with a chair, but others present gave a different account. The upshot of the affair was that Harland was seized by deputies, arrested on the spot, and charged with assault and battery. His reputation as an attorney was battered more severely than the client, however, and though he eventually beat the charge, the incident pretty well destroyed his practice. The Sanders temper had struck again.

There was probably never a time in his life when it would have been accurate to say that Harland Sanders was beaten, but there were times when he was down, and this was one of them. He was now thirty-one years old. He had been working for twenty years as farmhand, streetcar employee, soldier, section hand, blacksmith's helper, and fireman, and had enjoyed some success in the law. But he had encountered repeated failure largely through bullheadedness, a lack of self-control, impatience, and a self-righteous lack of diplomacy. Now he was jobless, with a wife and three children, and just about out of money.

He did the only thing he knew to do. He packed Josephine and the children off to her parents in Jasper, then he and Clarence, who, as Harland lamented, was "boozing himself to death," caught a train for Louisville, Kentucky, heading back for Indiana and the possibility of jobs with some of their kinfolk. Being short of funds, they "rode the blinds," crouching in the open-air space between the cars of a passenger train where they could gain free passage without being spotted by the brakeman. On their way north, the weather turned cold and they arrived in Louisville frozen stiff.

"I had to find Clarence a job," Harland said later. "Before we left Little Rock, he tried to talk me into being a hobo with him, bum around, don't you see? He was boozing bad, and I knew if I didn't get him something to do, he'd be back at it, gone again."

Through one of the Dunlevys, who always seemed to pop up at opportune moments, Harland learned that the village of New Washington, Indiana, had lost its only barber, and that the men there were getting a little shaggy. He found some secondhand barbershop equipment in a Louisville storage house, hauled it to New Washington in a secondhand Franklin he managed to buy on time, and set Clarence up in business. Clarence approached his new profession with some uncertainty, pointing out that he had never cut hair before, but Harland dismissed this as a minor handicap. "Don't think about it," he advised. "Just cut off what's too long and put on plenty of tonic. Their wives will like the way it smells and tell them they got a good cut." Apparently, the short course in barbering was sufficient. Clarence lit into the long-haired gentry with energy, if nothing else, and soon was serving a large and apparently satisfied clientele. In time he became a popular fixture in town, was self-supporting and respected, though there was some talk that he nipped occasionally at the tonic.

Harland didn't do as well. He couldn't find a job, and finally stooped once more to becoming a lowly section hand.

"Got a job with the Pennsylvania Railroad," he recounted. "Job driving spikes and laying rail. Drove spikes every foot of the way from Sellersburg to Scottsburg [Indiana]. Ten hours a day for $1.65 a day, and if we were twenty miles out in the country at the end of the ten hours, the foreman made us work till the last minute and then pump a handcar home."

The $1.65 a day, he soon saw, was not going to let him set anything aside for the family, so he took a job at night, after his ten-hour stint driving spikes, unloading coal cars at a local mill. He got $6.00 unloading a car holding from thirty to forty tons. He often worked past midnight, slept a few hours, and was back pounding steel by seven in the morning. It was a body-breaking routine, but he could put a little money away, and send some to Josephine, along with assurances that he would soon send for her and the children. He did not want to have to plan another kidnapping. Years later, when he was racked by the pain of arthritis, he wondered if some of it didn't trace back to those years of drudgery.

Actually, he no longer had cause to worry. Josephine and the children were comfortable at the King home in Jasper. Josephine had lost her earlier doubts about Harland's dependability. She knew that, whatever else he was, he was a worker, and she was confident that in time he would be sending for them.

And Harland was getting on his feet again. When he visited his relatives on weekends, and saw them sitting around on the porch in their suits and white shirts, he began to rebel against his lot as a manual laborer. His old self-confidence returned. After all, he thought, he had been a white-collar man himself, a lawyer, a professional man. He was "just as smart as them fellows," and he determined to leave the blue-collar ranks. He had heard from the front-porch grapevine that the Prudential Life Insurance Company was looking for a salesman, the last one having quit in disgust. With the money earned in a week of unloading coal, he bought a dignified gray suit and a pair of black shoes and presented himself at the Jeffersonville offices of Prudential Life, announcing that they were looking at "the best insurance salesman in the state of Indiana." Impressed with his brassy approach and convincing manner, the regional supervisor hired him.

He soon understood why his predecessor had quit. His territory was known as "graveyard territory," the toughest in the district, dimly regarded for the number of policyholders who were in arrears in their premium payments and the general poverty of the residents. Harland tore into it, as he put it, "like a possum after persimmons." He wheedled and threatened payments out of delinquents. He devised a scheme in which he would work his way through a neighborhood as "a representative of a firm conducting a survey" (of what, he didn't say). One of the questions he asked, of course, was whether the household was blessed with the protection of life insurance. If it was not, he returned the next day to give the family that opportunity. He did so well that within six months he was promoted to assistant supervisor, given a salary of $17.50 a week plus commissions, and transferred to the industrial insurance office.

Harland Sanders was not only a natural salesman, but a persistent one, and in the industrial division he again did well. At the end of thirteen months, he was transferred back to the ordinary life office, and this time given a whole division. But here, once more, he showed that the old Sanders bullheadedness had not succumbed to time or experience. When he turned in his report before leaving the industrial office, he was told to turn in his collections as well, so that the divisional accounts would be straight. Just as he had refused to release his Little Rock client's damage check until he got his fee, now he refused to turn in his accounts until he was paid his commissions. Again an argument ensued, although this time no one attacked him with a chair. Instead, he was fired.

But by this time, he had become known in the insurance community, and he quickly found another job, this time across the Ohio River in Louisville, selling for Mutual Benefit Life of New Jersey. He and Josephine, who had come north to join him when he went to work for Prudential, rented a comfortable home in Jeffersonville, and he became an active member of the local Young Businessmen's Club, and assumed a leading role in helping to organize their annual picnic. As part of the promotion, the young businessmen were urging all local business houses to close on the afternoon of the picnic, and when one barber declined, Harland went to see him. A customer was in the barber's chair, lathered up for a shave, and when Harland kept insisting that the barber cooperate in the picnic, the customer raised his head and expressed a very negative opinion of the picnic and its organizers. Harland replied with a negative opinion of the customer, whom he had never met, and the customer came out of the chair swinging. The fight boiled out of the shop and onto the street, where bystanders and a passing policeman kept it from reaching a decisive conclusion. Not knowing that his opponent was Jack Delanty, known as the town bully, Harland continued to express poor opinions of him and insist that he be allowed to teach the man a lesson. This won him some admiration from onlookers, created a lot of gossip, and aroused publicity that helped to make the picnic a big success. For once the Sanders temper had yielded some benefit.

But soon Harland began to tire of the insurance business. He began to look for greener pastures. Jeffersonville and New Albany were growing, and so was traffic between them and Louisville, across the Ohio River. But people on the Indiana side could get to Louisville only by going down to New Albany and taking the Kentucky and Indiana Railway Bridge, which afforded a two-lane road along with the rail lines. There was also a balky and irregular ferry nicknamed "Old Asthma." But automobiles, which had been almost a novelty a decade earlier, were now clogging the bridge and backing up in numbers the ferry could not handle. Harland spotted an opportunity.

Quickly forming a ferryboat company, he announced the start of construction on a steel-hulled, stern-wheel steamboat that would carry 15 cars and 150 people for ten cents a person, fifty cents a car. He had hit on a good idea. Within thirty days, he had sold enough stock to finance the venture, and his commission came to a neat $22,000. There was some muttering about the size of the commission, but the ferryboat was needed, and proved an immediate financial success when it went into service, returning a nice profit to its stockholders. And suddenly Harland was a substantial member of the business community.

The Roaring Twenties were under way. The United States had emerged from World War I as the new giant among the giant nations of the world, and Americans were giddy with their feelings of power and importance, confident that there were no limits to the industrial might of their system, sold on their belief that the sky was the limit. It was a time of explosive business growth, and businessmen who made money were regarded as proof of the essential rightness of American capitalism, especially when they made a lot of money. Harland was asked to join the Rotary Club, an acknowledgment of his acceptance by the business community. It was a proud moment for him. He remained an ardent Rotarian throughout his life, and maintained that he was always guided by Rotary's Four-Way Test for business conduct: Is it the truth? Is it fair to all concerned? Will it build goodwill and better friendships? Will it be beneficial to all concerned?

But his success had a strange outcome. His foray into the business world had convinced him that his future lay in business, and he concluded that the best way to get into business was to become involved in the business center of a thriving community. So when he learned that the chamber of commerce in Columbus, Indiana, was looking for an executive secretary, he applied and got the job. But it did not pan out as he had hoped. Columbus was an industrial town dominated by a few manufacturing plants. It presented few opportunities for an ambitious entrepreneur. The salary was not handsome, and he soon saw that it offered no real future. He quit.

Harland was again haunted by the specter of failure. He wanted painfully to be a success, and felt sure that he could be if he could find the right undertaking. He was thirty-three years old, and felt that he had to do something fast. He decided to strike out on his own.

For the first time in his hurried, restless life, he took some time out to mull over his situation and plan his future. Success, he concluded, the large-scale success of which he had begun to dream, came to the man who had the nerve and imagination to make things that people needed or wanted. And America in 1923, for all its booming steel mills, auto plants, coal mines, and shipyards, was still predominantly rural and agricultural. Most Americans still lived on farms. Huge fortunes had been made selling combines, threshers, and balers to farmers. He would make something the farmer needed. He took the money left from his ferryboat venture, rented an old warehouse in Jeffersonville, and began manufacturing acetylene lamps to replace the old dim kerosene lanterns that still lighted most farm homes.

It was a good idea, but it had come at the wrong time in the wrong place. First of all, his salesmen concentrated on the region of southern Indiana close to home, but it was a region of small farmers, many of them tenants whose income was precarious at best; those who bought soon fell behind in their payments. On top of that, just as Harland was beginning to get a foothold in the market, Delco came out with a compact power plant that enabled the solid farmer to have electricity on his farm even when he had no access to utility power lines. Harland couldn't sell the farmers who could pay, and those he could sell couldn't pay. His lamp venture collapsed. He had lost his investment. Once more, he was without business, job, or income.

He was not beaten, but he was depressed. All around him were signs of an unprecedented prosperity. Successful businessmen were building fine homes, taking vacations, even going abroad. The business mentality of Sinclair Lewis' *Main Street* was in full flower. The Jazz Age, fueled by bootleg whiskey that openly ignored the pathetic aims of Prohibition, set the tone of the times. Flappers, symbolizing the new, free, adventurous spirit, rode in rumble seats, smoked cigarettes, danced to the wail of saxophones, and frequented speakeasies. Broadway, the Great White Way, blazed with light and boomed with the sound of *Follies* and *Scandals*. The daughters of American millionaires went abroad to bring home titled husbands. Stockbrokers built mansions, and the stock market became the new magical game that led to the end of the rainbow. Every day in every way, America was getting better and better—and richer and richer.

And Harland Sanders was missing the parade. He was convinced that he had shown the energy, the ability, and the imagination that should have yielded riches. But somehow, his dreams eluded him.

Resignedly, he went back into the life insurance business, once more selling for Mutual Benefit Life in Louisville, but his hardest job was selling himself, convincing himself each morning that he could still use the insurance premium as a stepping-stone to success. It was a lackluster performance. Within a few weeks, he heard that the Michelin Tire Company in Louisville was looking for a salesman. He hurried to apply, made his usual hard-hitting presentation, and became the Michelin representative, with all of Kentucky as his sales territory. He had a simple explanation for his switch from insurance to tires.

"Well, for one thing, everybody was going car crazy," he said. "Even people who didn't need one were getting one. And there were four wheels on every one of them, and every wheel had to have a tire.

"Now, in insurance you had to go out and dig up your prospect and then sell him, and then see that he paid his premiums. But every car was my prospect, and with Michelin I had a guarantee of $750 a month, which was mighty good money then. Well, I didn't exactly have a guarantee of $750. I had a guarantee of $750 if I made my quota, but naturally I always made my quota. I established dealerships all over the state, as well as selling tires myself, and then I humped them to keep the tires moving."

Coaxing his old Franklin across Kentucky's rough roads, he tried to establish dealerships anywhere that cars, gasoline, or farm equipment was sold, and he began earning more than his $750 a month. He traded the old Franklin in on a $1,600 Maxwell. He and Josephine rented a comfortable home in Winchester, a small town twenty miles east of Lexington, which he felt was nearer the center of the state and therefore a better base of operations, though it also reflected the fact that he never liked to live in a large town. Life was beginning to look good again.

One day, driving near the Camp Nelson community in Jessamine County, south of Lexington, he noticed a small white house sitting on a rise at the foot of a hill where Jessamine Creek joined the Kentucky River. The land around it looked rich and clean. He bought it. He was now a man with a family, a home, a good job, and a fine car. Fate was smiling again.

He and Josephine enjoyed their home on Jessamine Creek. He fixed up the barn and used it as a site for what he termed "big feeds," to which he invited his tire dealers from around the state. Sometimes the parties would last all afternoon and into the night, to the tune of country music and square dancing. Whether or not the public relations paid off did not bother him greatly. He was having a good time.

One reason for his enjoyment of the job was that it gave him a chance to indulge his flair for showmanship to the hilt, and he loved it. During the twenties, small-town Kentucky was devoted to special Saturdays, called Court Day, Mule Day, or something of the kind, when farmers poured into the county seat to gossip, visit, buy, sell, and swap their produce and artifacts. During most of the year, there was usually a special day somewhere in the state, and Harland used them to good advantage. Putting on his ribbed "tire" or "bib" suit, the kind used in Michelin ads, he would stride through the courthouse square, challenging all the local tire dealers to a contest which, he promised, would show the superiority of the Michelin tire.

Actually, it was a test of inner tube rather than tire. Harland would challenge the dealer of a rival brand to a contest to see whether his inner tube or the Michelin tube would burst first. Two husky farm boys would be asked to pump away, and the crowd invited to count the strokes each boy used to inflate the tubes. As the inner tubes grew in size, finally bulging at the point of least strength in a great bubble, Harland would keep up a running spiel, warning his onlookers to stand back from the rival tire lest it burst and lash them with rubber. By the time the first tire exploded, a big crowd was usually watching, and the Michelin, being a quality tube, invariably won the contest. It was wonderful advertising for Harland's product. It wasn't long before word got around and competitive dealers refused to cooperate in his scheme.

He then devised another, if less spectacular, demonstration, asking the onlookers to guess how many strokes of the pump it would take to inflate the inner tube to the bursting point, sometimes giving away a small prize (or a discount on a tire) to the person making the best guess.

"We'd start pumping the dern thing and it would grow bigger than a beer keg before it would finålly burst," he recalled later. The noise of the bursting tube was always accompanied by shrieks and laughter from the audience. Harland was learning how to attract and hold a crowd. He was also selling a lot of tires and inner tubes. And he was discovering something about himself which he had only sensed before. He could get people's attention. He could make them listen to him. He could influence them. He became convinced that somewhere within himself there was a natural leader of men. Maybe, he thought, he was meant for great things.

4

While the Sanders family was living at Camp Nelson, Harland Jr. had to drive himself and his sisters to school each morning in the Model A Ford his father had gotten him. Harland was gone too much of the time to take them, and Nicholasville, where they went to school, was too far—about seven miles—for them to walk. And in 1924 there was nothing unusual about a thirteen-year-old boy driving. Farm boys drove from the time they were physically able to handle machinery. They couldn't be properly useful otherwise. They drove tractors on the farm and on the highway. They drove farm trucks into town to deliver produce and get supplies. There was a massive outcry when, following World War II, the state finally clamped down on underaged and unlicensed drivers. Many simply ignored the law.

So it was taken for granted that Harland Jr. would drive to school. But on the Monday before Thanksgiving, his Ford refused to start. Father and son tried vainly to coax it to life.

Finally Harland hitched it to his Maxwell coupé with a rope
and began to tow it to a garage. But they had to cross a rickety
bridge over Jessamine Creek not far from their home, and
Harland was out on the bridge only a few feet when it collapsed, dropping his car about forty feet, where it landed on
its top with the front end underwater. Harland Jr.'s car was
pulled after it, but the rope broke and the Ford fell only a few
feet onto the bank, stopping before it reached the creek.

Harland Jr. had only a cut thumb to show for the experience, but his father's plight was far more serious. The fall had
crushed the car's top and the driver's side was split wide open.
The driver's seat was mostly underwater. Harland was cut and
stunned when he was thrown against the windshield, but by
diving through the broken side of the car, he managed to fight
free and clamber up the bank, soaked and covered with mud
and blood.

Blood was pouring down his face and into his eyes. His scalp
had been split from his forehead to the top of his skull, and he
could feel a flap of it hanging down over one ear. While he
was fighting, confused and battered, to get out of the flooded
car, he had swallowed water, and was coughing and retching
as he tried to climb up the slippery bank.

Harland Jr. had jumped from his Ford before it came to
rest, relatively undamaged, against a small tree, and now he
scrambled down the bank to help his father, and together they
made it back to the shattered bridge. His shouts had attracted
a small group of people from a nearby store. When they saw
Harland, muddy and bleeding, they began shouting for someone to call a doctor. Harland was having none of it.

"You wait till I say get a doctor before you go getting any
doctor," he croaked, and, taking his split scalp in his hands, he
pressed it back in place.

"I just took my two hands and pushed it back together, you
see, and held it there, with the blood squishing, until it dried,"
he said. "Held it together firm and the blood dried in just a few
minutes. Grew back as pretty as anything. It didn't look good.

It was two or three weeks before I could wash it, and I had to wear a hat, don't you see, but there never was any scar, except now when it gets cold you can see where it was. Turns sort of blue, don't you see?"

But he had suffered more than a split scalp. The Maxwell was a total wreck; by the time he got it out of the creek, he sold it for thirty-five dollars. This hurt worse than the cuts and bruises, for without a car he could not hope to do his job.

But there are puzzling aspects of this incident that Harland never quite explained. Until the accident, he had been the owner of a home and two cars, a man with a good job and some savings. He could surely have borrowed the money for a new car. He could have used his son's Ford, which was soon repaired. Yet for some reason, he did not get another car, at least not immediately, and a week after the accident took a bus to call on one final customer in order to meet his monthly quota. Then he left the company.

It is possible that Michelin had warned him that it was planning to cut back its nonmetropolitan operations, and that he decided to get out while the going was good. Beginning in 1929 Michelin did, in fact, cut back sharply, and in 1932, with the Depression slashing its tire business, ended its U.S. operations entirely, moving its manufacturing facilities back to France. But the Depression was something not dreamed of in the winter of 1924–25.

In any event, by Christmas of 1924 Harland was no longer a Michelin representative, and shortly after the first of the year he hitchhiked to Louisville to look for a job. Why he hitchhiked instead of taking the bus is one of those questions about Harland Sanders that defies answer. He was surely not broke. But throughout his life, and often for no reason at all, he was given to fits of unusual penny-pinching, especially when things were going wrong or he was suffering bad luck.

Now, once more, his roller coaster headed uphill. He caught a ride with a man who introduced himself as Mr. Gardner, a division manager for Standard Oil of Kentucky. Harland, always a ready talker, soon poured out the story of his misfortunes, including the fact that he was looking for a job.

"Mr. Gardner asked me if I thought I could run a filling station," he recalled, "and I said, 'No reason I couldn't,' and he said he thought he could get me a good deal on a filling station in Nicholasville that they had. They had a man running it they weren't too pleased with; seems he wasn't doing the job, working at it, so he asked me if I would like to try it. So I said, 'I sure would.' So a week later, I took over this Standard station in Nicholasville. I figured living only a few miles away at Camp Nelson and with my children going to school there, I knew the town and the region pretty good, and it looked like a good deal."

Nicholasville, a quiet, pretty, county-seat town of three thousand people, was a pleasant place to live. Located in the center of Jessamine County, an area of small but substantial farms, and situated on U. S. Highway 27, it was only a dozen miles from Lexington, the heart of the prosperous bluegrass region. Crowds of local people regularly attended University of Kentucky football and basketball games in Lexington, hundreds of farmers came into Nicholasville on Saturdays, and there was considerable through traffic on US 27. Harland's new station was located right on Main Street to take advantage of it. After selling his place at Camp Nelson, he bought a white frame house across the street from the station, from which the children could easily walk to school. He seemed to be well fixed.

But his first weeks at his new station were not easy. The former operator, a man named Lane, was popular in town, and his old customers resented it when he was replaced. Nearby Lake Herrington, created by construction of the Dix River Dam, was just filling in 1925, and the people of Nicholasville were excited over the new recreational area. The fishing was good. Dozens of boat docks, ramps, fishing lodges, and vacation cabins were springing up around the lake, and Lane had been spending more time fishing, tinkering with boats, and

talking about the future of the lake than on the filling station.
But the townspeople shared this enthusiasm, objected to his
removal, and avoided the station when Harland took over. In
his first week, he pumped just three and a half gallons of gas.

But Harland was determined and, for once, patient. Furthermore, he had some ideas about how a filling station should
be run, and he was eager to try them out. He cleaned the
place, inside and out, until it sparkled. He put up a new sign.
And he began to give service of a kind the people had not seen
before. A few years before, while traveling for Michelin, he
had pulled into a filling station in Portsmouth, Ohio, where the
attendant had wiped off his windshield without being asked. It
made an impression on him, and now he suspected it would
impress others. He started wiping windshields as part of the
service. And he gave away air and checked tires without being
asked. He made a bit thing of the free air, even put up a big
sign: FREE AIR. In a sense, it was a gimmick, but it was also
good public relations. Business picked up.

"Within six months, we were pumping more gas than any
station in Kentucky. The people in the Louisville office used to
bring new men down to see how I did it, told them to use their
heads, their imaginations, like I was doing," he boasted.

The children liked living in town. So did Josephine, though
she was not by nature a gregarious woman. Aside from his
service station, Harland rented a storage building where the
city hall now stands and operated it as a parking garage. Once
more, he was making money, sharing the prosperity of the
twenties. He quickly became part of the local business community. His station became something of a loafing place. Old-
timers recall that "Sanders was a great talker. You could always go down there and he would be arguing with somebody
about something."

Not that this apparently comfortable life mellowed him
much.

"Sanders was a nice fellow," recalls Albert McDowell, who
was a merchant in Nicholasville at the time. "And he was

popular, one of the boys, you know? There was always a
bunch hanging around, loafing, talking. But he was a hothead.
Fly off the handle at anything.

"There was this restaurant down the street from his place,
Baskett's, real nice place, and Baskett always kept everything
nice and clean. Kept things very pretty. And one day Sanders
went down and told the man at the counter there that he had
the heartburn and could he have a glass of water with some
baking soda in it. The man gave it to him and he drank it and
started out, and Fred Baskett said to him, 'That'll be five cents,
Sanders.' Well, Sanders had a fit. 'Five cents?' he hollered.
'Hell's fire, I can buy a whole box of soda for five cents!'
Baskett said to him, 'Well, you didn't. You drank mine. And
you owe me five cents.'

"Well, one of them called the other a cheapskate, and the
other called him a skinflint, and the first thing you know
Sanders reached over and hit him right in the face. Baskett
picked up a sugar bowl, not a bowl but one of those glass
jars with a metal top that you shake sugar out of, and threw it
at him. Sanders ducked, and the bowl went right through the
glass of the front door. And Sanders threw down a nickel and
said, 'All right. There. Buy yourself a new door, you cheap
sonofabitch!' "

On another occasion, a man who parked regularly in the
garage came in one morning but found the garage floor
flooded with oily water from a leaking pipe, and refused to get
out of his car. Harland apologized, promised to have the water
cleaned up shortly, and offered to pay the man's cost of parking somewhere else. The following day the man returned to
find the water still on the floor and said to Harland, "How do
you expect a man to park in a pigpen like this?" Harland
didn't like to hear his place called a pigpen, and told the man
that if he didn't like it he didn't have to come in there. One
word led to another, and after an exchange of insults, the man
jumped out of his car and a fight began. The man knocked
Harland down; Harland grabbed a piece of concrete and hit
him with it, breaking his leg. That didn't build goodwill.

But, in all, they were good years. Though some people regarded him as a bigmouth and a hothead, Harland was popular. His success and the respect of company officials restored his confidence. He was making money and his family was well cared for. And he was with a big company, one with which, he began to hope, he might go far.

But storm clouds were gathering over the Kentucky countryside. Long before the stock market crash of 1929 sent warnings of the approaching Depression across the nation, farm prices had begun to slide, while prices of farm equipment and supplies rose in response to the industrial boom. Then a ruinous drought hit central Kentucky.

Small farmers, caught between rising costs and falling prices for their produce, began laying off help. Grocery and feed stores, hardware and clothing stores soon felt the drop in buying, and they too began laying off employees. Lexington, blessed with tobacco warehouses and drying plants, distilleries, colleges, and big horse farms—none of which suffered greatly during the Great Depression—continued to be prosperous, and more and more men started heading up US 27 to look for work. As the weeks passed, business at the Standard station went slowly downhill. More and more men drifted by, looking for work or asking for a loan to tide them over. The parking garage was practically empty.

"Just as business was going good, things just sorta caved in," Harland lamented. "Business fell off to nothing. That drought hit us hard. I saw farmers selling sheep for fifty cents they had paid thirty-five dollars for, just so somebody could get them to water. We just dried up. There wasn't a farm pond in the county with enough water to drown a cat in. Lexington was down to two days' supply before they finally got a line through from the Kentucky River.

"We just went busted. It was like things was just dying around us. Every day you'd hear about somebody going busted, see some store close down. Didn't see nobody on the streets but children, and men looking for work. I did everything I knew to keep going, doing all the work myself. But nothing I could do could give people the money to buy. I sold my grease rack, finally, for next to nothing, just to pay the rent. But it was no go. I had to give it up."

His situation was now far more serious than on the other occasions when he had found himself out of work. He was almost forty years old. He had a family to support, and that was becoming more expensive. In 1928, Margaret had been accepted at Berea College, in nearby Berea, Kentucky. Berea was established during the middle of the nineteenth century by abolitionist ministers to provide an education for poor children of the Appalachian region, white and black alike. Kentucky's Day Law, passed by the legislature shortly before World War I, had forbidden the education of white and black students under a common roof, but the school continued to flourish and provide a Christian education for deserving students from the Appalachian area. It was a no-nonsense college, with strict rules, demanding academic standards, and a requirement that all students work. All of these appealed to Harland and Josephine, and though they lived outside the Appalachian region, they managed to get Margaret admitted (Mildred would soon follow). As out-of-territory students, however, the girls could not live in the school dormitories, so Josephine moved to Berea and rented an apartment, where she and the girls lived during most of the year.

Whether this was necessary is questionable. If Harland could get the girls admitted as out-of-territory students, it is likely that he could have gotten them a dormitory room, had he wanted badly enough to make the effort. The fact seems to be that Josephine was more than happy to live separately in Berea with the girls, and that Harland was just as happy to have her there.

A worse-matched pair would be hard to find. Harland was gregarious, hot-tempered, and emotional, a man who loved to talk, show off, and make grand gestures. His eyes flamed with fury one moment, filled with tears the next. But he longed to be lover as well as fighter, and Josephine would not satisfy this part of the marriage agreement. As long as he lived, Harland

Sanders loved women; he could not come into a room without touching, patting, hugging any available woman. Josephine, on the other hand, was a cool, taciturn, withdrawn woman who found her husband's physical demands unbearable. If he later gained a reputation for philandering, it is no great surprise. He was acutely lonely much of the time.

By the beginning of 1930, the Depression was settling like a gray blight across the land that only months before had believed that its prosperity would never end. And Harland now found himself one of the growing army of unemployed that would soon claim one of every four adult males. But the good work he had done at his Nicholasville station, and the reputation it had earned him, would soon pay dividends.

U.S. Highway 25, running from Lexington through Corbin and on to the south, had just been completed, with a branch, 25E, extending from Corbin through the Cumberland Gap to the east, and Shell Oil officials decided that the location could support a station despite the Depression. They had heard of Harland's work in Nicholasville, and in the summer of 1930 offered to give him their Corbin station rent-free. He would pay a penny a gallon extra in lieu of rent.

"Naturally," said Harland, "I grabbed at it and went to Corbin. It was a bigger town than Nicholasville, and business was better. It was a railroad town, mainly, with a Southern shop and yards, and some coal business. And it was right on the north-south road, US 25. It was a rough town then, too."

Corbin was, indeed, a sharp contrast to placid, farm-oriented, bluegrass Nicholasville. Located on the northern border of Whitley County, it lay in the foothills of the eastern Kentucky mountains that had earned a bloody, if colorful, reputation as the spawning ground of mine wars, moonshine whiskey, bootlegging, and pistol justice. Corbin itself was a bustling town of six thousand people, with its quota of churches and civic clubs, and a booster spirit reflected in its chamber of commerce.

But North Corbin, where Harland's new station was located on a shallow curve a short distance from the junction of US 25 and US 25E, shared few of these virtues. Lying just across the county line in Laurel County, it was a roadside sprawl of small stores, filling stations, modest homes, and establishments suspected of selling illegal liquor. During Prohibition, these unlawful oases peddled, usually at prices ranging from twenty-five to fifty cents a pint, the famed and vicious white moonshine corn whiskey boiled off in illicit stills back in the hills. Fights between consumers of this potent liquor were frequent and often deadly.

Partly out of the need for self-defense, partly because of the mountain tradition of gun-toting, many of the residents of North Corbin carried pistols. Practically everyone had a gun in the house or at the store. Miners, railroad workers, and rural toughs brawled on weekends, while deputies tried to restrain the high-spirited and Internal Revenue agents tried vainly to stop the flow of illegal spirits. No one seemed to give much thought to the flow of businessmen, salesmen, and tourists on US 25. It would be years before the city fathers realized their potential value to the local economy. To the suspicious, xenophobic rural dwellers, tourists were outsiders, a bad thing. Others saw the traffic as a strange nuisance. It was into this environment that Harland moved in the summer of 1930.

His location was not the best. The station just across the road was more visible to drivers approaching from either direction. But Harland determined to overcome the handicap by employing his old trade-boosting tactics. He again put up his signs offering free air. He offered to wipe windshields and check tires. He put in an air compressor, shined his pumps, and swept his driveway religiously.

"Fellow named Ancel McVey had the station just across the road from mine," Harland recalled. "He had a better location than mine. The road curved then, and when you came down the road, there his place was and you could see it for a long way, either way you were coming. As nice a fellow as you would want to meet, but he didn't work at his station much, not much of a hustler. Spent a lot of time playing the mandolin. He could play it, too. Fellows would come down there of an evening or on weekends, you know, and bring a guitar or a fiddle and they would play. And he had this hog, sort of a pet, don't you see, that he kept right there at the station, and he kept this puddle full of water for the hog to wallow in. I coulda told him it didn't look too good.

"I put in this air compressor to give folks air, you see, the only one around, and when they came to put the line in, I had them dig a little trench across the road and run a line over so McVey could have air too, free. That made a hit with him. We got along good. When he decided to quit, he let me have his place for twenty-five dollars a month, and later sold it to me reasonable."

Unlike McVey, Harland worked. And he watched his pumps.

"When a fellow pulled in, he didn't want to sit there waiting," he said. "And he didn't want to have to go looking for somebody to wait on him. And he didn't want some greasy, dirty fellow coming out to wait on him. I made a point of being neat, you see, clean."

But within months after he began his new venture, tragedy struck the Sanders family. Harland Jr. began complaining of a sore throat, and a visit to the doctor showed that he had infected, swollen tonsils. Harland took him to the hospital in Richmond, Kentucky, fifty-five miles north of Corbin, where the tonsils were removed. It was a simple operation, but the young man seemed to recover very slowly. He was weak, nervous, and had no appetite. With Josephine and the girls in Berea, there was no one but Harland to look after him, and Harland had to spend most of his time at the station. So after a few days, he took him to a health resort in Martinsville, Indiana, to rest. On the way, he stopped off to see his mother, who was now back in Henryville, following the death of her husband.

He then went on to Martinsville, where he left Harland Jr., after making arrangements to come back for him in a week. But on his way back to Martinsville the following week, he stopped again to see his mother and found her in tears. "Oh, Harland," she said, "you poor boy. Your son is dead." The people in Martinsville had tried to reach Harland to tell him personally, but he had already left Corbin, and they had learned his mother's address from the man running the station during Harland's absence.

In Martinsville, the doctor who had attended young Harland explained to his father that the boy had apparently picked up a streptococcus in the hospital, blood poisoning had set in, and he had developed blood clots, one of which killed him. Harland took him back to Henryville and buried him.

He tried as best he could to console Josephine for the loss of their only son, but by this time she and Harland were too remote to be of much comfort to each other. The loss of the boy cut them both deeply. Years later, when he had built and then sold a food empire, Harland would often and bitterly complain to friends that he would not have had to sell if young Harland had been alive.

Back in Corbin, Harland decided that his station needed a little promotion. He began advertising—not in the usual way, of course. He began with the sides of barns.

"This traveling painter came by one day looking for work so he could buy food," he said. "I told him if he was working for peanuts, I couldn't pay him a shell, but he kept hanging around and pretty soon we worked out a deal. Shell furnished the paint, and I'd go out and paint the side of a barn red, and this fellow would come along behind me and letter in the sign. I'll tell you, those signs helped. My gas business almost doubled."

Asked why he used signs on the sides of barns rather than the usual signboards, Harland explained that local hunters and good old boys riding around full of liquor shot up signboards as fast as a man could put them up.

"But if they knew there might be a mule or a cow in the barn behind that sign, they wouldn't blast away with a shotgun or take out their pistol and try to put a hole in the *o* or dot the *i* the way they liked to."

Harland was well aware of the local residents' propensity for firearms. And they used them on more than signboards. The North Corbin area had earned the name of "Hell's Half-Acre," though it covered considerably more land than that, mainly because of the frequent gunplay. Even after Prohibition was repealed, Corbin remained dry, and shooting was not uncommon in the blind tigers along US 25. Harland himself kept a pistol on a shelf beneath his cash register, and what he referred to as a "hawg rifle," but which was actually an ordinary shotgun, in his bedroom. He might never have used the pistol had it not been for his advertising campaign.

About a half-mile south of Harland's Shell station, US 25 was flanked by a concrete wall forming an embankment along the L&N Railroad Line. It was highly visible to traffic, so Harland decided to use it as a signboard. The sign he had painted was simply a large arrow, pointing north, with the words NORTH TO LEXINGTON on the arrow. There was no direct mention of his station, but the directions led traffic past his station. They also diverted traffic past the station of a competitor, Matt Stewart, who had a short time before opened a Standard Oil station down the road. Matt Stewart, said people around North Corbin, "wasn't a man to be messed with." He was known to own a gun, and said to be willing to fight, with the gun or with his fists. He did not take kindly to the sign, and insisted that it was illegal, since it was painted on railroad property to which Harland had no right. (Actually, the railroad seemed not to care, and officials testified later that they had neither permitted nor forbidden the sign.)

Harland first scented trouble when a local truck driver stopped and told him that Matt Stewart had painted over his sign. He found that Stewart had not only painted over the sign, but had done so with creosote, which was hard to remove and impossible to paint over. He got some rags and gasoline and, after scrubbing off the creosote, repainted the sign and paid a social call on Matt Stewart. Differing accounts were given later of what transpired, but either Sanders or Stewart, or both, promised to "blow your goddam head off" if there was more sign activity. Harland said Stewart threatened him. Stewart swore that Harland had both cursed and threatened him.

At any rate, bad blood developed between the two men. On

the morning of May 7, 1931, just after he opened the station, Harland was visited by Robert Gibson, the Shell Oil district manager out of Middlesboro, and H. D. Shelburne, a Shell supervisor. As the three men stood outside the station talking, a boy came running up and said, "Hey, Sanders, Matt Stewart's painting over your sign again." Harland told the two men about his trouble with Stewart, and the three of them decided to see Stewart and have it out with him. They got into Gibson's car, with Shelburne driving, Gibson in the passenger seat, and Harland in back, and drove down to the sign. As they crossed the short bridge over Lynn Camp Creek, they could see Stewart on a ladder, busily painting out the arrow. Harland and Gibson got out as the car stopped.

"Well, you yellow dog," Harland yelled (at least that is what he said he yelled; it is likely he used stronger language). "I see you done it again." Stewart replied with an oath and jumped down from the ladder. Someone pulled a gun. Five shots sounded. Gibson fell, hit three times near the heart and once in an arm as he spun around from the impact of the bullets. As Gibson fell, Shelburne jumped from the driver's seat and opened fire on Stewart, who ran down the road and jumped behind a retaining wall. Harland later said that, as he bent over the fallen Gibson, he saw Gibson's pistol, which he grabbed and fired. Stewart testified that Harland pulled a pistol from his own pocket. The police concluded merely that "all of the men were armed."

Stewart, now flanked by Harland and Shelburne, crawled over the wall and started for Harland, who was crouched at the other end of the wall. Raising up, he saw Stewart coming toward him and fired, hitting Stewart in the shoulder, about the time Shelburne shot him in the hip.

"Don't shoot, Sanders!" Stewart cried. "You've killed me."

They hadn't killed him, but they had stopped him, and they stood over him, with guns drawn, until the police arrived, called to the scene by one of the men who had followed along to see the fight. Gibson was rushed to Edwards Hospital, but was dead on arrival. Stewart was painfully, but not fatally, wounded. He was arrested and charged with murder. Harland and Shelburne were arrested and charged with shooting with intent to kill. They posted bond and accompanied Gibson's body back to Middlesboro.

The charges against Harland and Shelburne were dismissed after a hearing. Stewart was tried, found guilty, and sentenced to eighteen years in prison. He was out on bond, pending an appeal of his conviction, when, two years later, he was shot and killed by Deputy Sheriff John Miles. Miles and his son had gone to Stewart's place of business to arrest a man working for him. When the younger Miles grabbed the man and tried to take him outside, he was jumped by Stewart. John Miles rushed to his son's aid. Stewart picked up a two-by-four. John Miles shot him dead. The case became the subject of great controversy. Many people in Corbin insisted that there was no cause for Miles to shoot Stewart, and even today some remember that, at the time, there were rumors that Miles had been paid by relatives of Robert Gibson to kill Stewart. The charges were never proved.

The incident was to have a strange aftermath for Harland. Stewart was survived by a daughter, Ona May. Unlike her hotheaded father, Ona May Stewart was an attractive, sensible girl, and a good student who later attended Union College in nearby Barbourville. After her father was killed, Harland apologized to her for his part in the tragedy, and offered to help her if he ever could. Later, he did.

In the meantime, Harland was working to put the shooting episode behind him and build his filling station business. He was little known at the time (indeed, the local paper, the Corbin *Times-Tribune*, in its account of the gunfight, listed him as "H. D. Saunders"), and there is no evidence that the publicity hurt him. Little by little, he developed a clientele of truck drivers and "drummers," as traveling salesmen were called. Many of them, as well as tourists, would ask Harland where they could get a good meal, and he would send them to one of the several eating places in town, though warning them not to expect too much. Then one day a salesman complained, "Damn! There ain't a decent place around here to eat."

"I'm afraid you're right, friend," Harland agreed. But the remark stuck in his mind, and after thinking about it, he decided that the problem presented an opportunity. No one, least of all Harland Sanders, realized at the time that the seed had been planted for America's fast-food revolution.

5

For a revolution, it had an unimpressive beginning.

"I got to thinking about it, don't you see, and it came to me that one thing I always could do was cook," said Harland, "and I figured I couldn't do worse than these people running these places around town. So, well, I had this little room off the main office, oh, about twelve by fifteen, that I used for storage. So I went downtown and bought this piece of linoleum, bought it to fit, smoothed off the rough planking, and laid it myself.

"I didn't have any money to buy furnishings, you know, so I just brought out the dining room table and chairs and put them out there, in that room. We had six chairs, but that was all the table would hold. And I started serving meals to anyone wanted them."

At first, the Sanders family lived in rooms behind the station. While the girls were in college, Harland ran the dining room operation by himself. When they came home, Josephine helped.

"We'd fix dinner—dinner was the noon meal then, you see—for the family, and if nobody came, we'd eat it. If people came, we'd have to fix more for the family."

When a driver would pull up and ask where he could get a decent meal, Harland would tell him, "Right here, friend, if you don't mind plain home cooking." And it was not fancy. It was boardinghouse-style. Harland put the bowls and platters of food in the middle of the table, and the diners helped themselves to as much as they wanted while it lasted. Truck drivers ate alongside salesmen and tourists heading for Florida. There was country ham, served with redeye gravy, or pot roast or fried chicken, mashed potatoes, fresh vegetables, and milk gravy, to go with the potatoes ("I always made my mashed potatoes light and fluffy, you know? I hate soggy potatoes"). And there was coffee and buttermilk, and home-baked pies. After they sampled it, customers decided they didn't mind the plain home cooking at all. Word of his food got around. It wasn't long before he had to bring out some armchairs, so that people could wait in some comfort.

"We didn't have much to start with," Harland recalled. "A stove with four burners, and an oven, and this refrigerator with the motor on top, you remember? That was about it."

Soon people were stopping who didn't want gas or oil, or even free air. Harland began to wish that he had more room. He put up a big sign, north of his filling station, saying SANDERS SHELL STATION AND CAFE. Later, he changed it to read SANDERS CAFE AND SERVICE STATION.

Harland was not content to be a filling station operator, or even the proprietor of a restaurant. He began to be more active in Corbin civic affairs, joined the local Rotary, became a member of the chamber of commerce and a Mason. He became a one-man lobby for the improvement of US 25, and of the neglected tourist business which, he was convinced, was an untapped gold mine. He railed at fellow Rotarians when they tended to take the tourist business lightly.

"The tourist business could be worth more to this town than

all the roundhouses the L&N and Southern could build," he told them. "But you sapsuckers are too goddam dumb to see it." Anything that interfered with the tourist flow through Corbin sent him into a fury, and this got him, once again, into trouble with the law.

The tourist traffic represented one kind of opportunity to Harland Sanders, and quite a different kind to local law enforcement officers. After listening to drivers' complaints, Harland became convinced that the local JPs were operating a well-oiled speed trap. The deputies arrested motorists by the handfuls and took them before the local justice of the peace, where they usually chose to pay the speeding fine rather than wait to be heard in a regular county court. He charged that the deputies and JPs split the fines, with a cut going to the county attorney.

To combat this, he had forms printed informing the arrested drivers that they could have the JP sworn off the bench, or ask for a change in venue to county court. Each day he would appear in the court of the justice of the peace and distribute these forms among the accused, many of whom followed his suggestion. He began making inroads on the racket's revenues. One day, as he was handing out his forms, he was accosted by a deputy.

"You're under arrest, Sanders," he was informed.

"What for?" he demanded.

"Practicing law without a license," he was told, whereupon he and four others were put into a deputy's car and driven toward the Laurel County seat in London.

Harland suspected that the whole thing was a shakedown, that the deputy had no intention in the world of taking them before the county judge, and was depending on them to weaken and pay their fines before reaching the courthouse. He told the others not to worry, and assured them that all would be well when they faced the county judge, who would see what a racket was being run. His suspicions grew when the deputy began to beg them to go ahead and pay the fine rather than face the embarrassment of being led into the courthouse, and run the risk of a heavier fine.

"Keep driving," Harland snapped. "We'll take our chances."

The deputy became increasingly nervous as they approached the county seat. Again he begged them to avoid the wait and the indignity. He offered to use his good offices to have their fines lessened if they would appear before the JP.

"Keep going," Harland told him.

Finally, the deputy turned around and drove back to North Corbin. Without a word, he stalked into the JP court, leaving them free to go. When Harland reported this to the chamber of commerce, local businessmen and officials finally took notice, appealed to the authorities of Laurel County, and the speed trap was abandoned. The event made him the target of deputies when he drove through Laurel County, but it enhanced his reputation in Corbin.

More important was Ancel McVey's decision, late in 1934, to quit his filling station and to rent it to Harland, who was tickled to get it. It was not only a better location, but had a big side room and a vacant lot on one side that would let him expand if he needed to. Harland bought a small bungalow on a side street near the station and threw himself into the job of remodeling his new station. He repainted the building, paved the driveway, put a plate glass window in the office, and turned the side room into a real restaurant, with six tables, each seating four to six people. And he filled in the hog puddle.

Harland was a good cook, a very good cook, with an instinct for flavor and appearance. But he didn't know anything about the restaurant business. He learned. At first, he or his waitress would simply recite to customers a list of the food available for the day, as was then customary in most small-town restaurants.

This didn't look good. It often proved unhandy. Customers would forget what he had recited to them and he would have to repeat it. Sometimes, to his embarrassment, he would forget what was available and have to go to the kitchen to check. He began offering printed menus, a novelty in the area, and soon decided they were worth the money. He also began to advertise, and before long he boasted the "biggest restaurant sign in Kentucky."

But running both the filling station and the restaurant was getting to be a load. Not only did Harland have to man the pumps, wipe windshields, check tires and batteries, sweep out cars, and give directions; he also planned menus, shopped or did the ordering, cooked, waited on tables, watched the cash register, and, when the day's business was done, cleaned the tables, scrubbed the floors, washed the dishes, pots, and pans, emptied the garbage, set the tables for breakfast, and checked supplies. He badly needed help, but with the Depression deepening every day, he worried about meeting a payroll. Finally, he had no choice. He hired his first waitress, Nell Ray.

"She wasn't my first employee," Harland explained. "The first was her husband, George Ray. He came into the station one day and said to me, 'Sanders, I just got to have some work to put some food on the table for my family, all there is to it.' Well, I felt for him. There was lots of good folks then just plain going hungry, but I had to tell him I didn't have any money to pay him. He said he'd work for any food that was left over, and he kept hanging around, doing little jobs here and there, things that needed doing, and after a couple of weeks I couldn't let him go. So when the lunchroom got going and I was looking for a waitress, he said his wife would do the job and I hired her."

Curiously, hiring Nell Ray proved to be one of the most far-reaching things Harland ever did, though not because Nell was a competent waitress and part-time cook. During the last week of October 1932, she got sick and couldn't make it to work, and asked her twin sister, Claudia, to take her place. Claudia was looking for work, and said sure.

Born in the Cane Creek section of Knox County, Kentucky, in 1902, one of fourteen children born to Jerry and Nancy Leddington, Claudia was under no illusions that life was a bed of roses. At nineteen, she had married Charles Price, and they had moved to Knoxville, Tennessee, where their first child, Elvis Ray, was born. But the marriage soured and, pregnant, she moved back to Kentucky and went to live with her parents in North Corbin until the second child, Billie Jean, was born. Then Claudia started looking for work.

"I always liked to hire widows with children because they needed the work and there wasn't any foolishness about them," Harland said frankly, and Claudia, although not actually a widow, seemed to fit the bill. Calm, tough, and sensible, she was not put off by either the work or by Harland's famed temper.

"We started in a mighty small way, you know," she said later. "It's hard to remember exactly what I thought of him. He seemed nice and friendly. Oh, he had a temper. He had that. But he didn't take it out on me. Oh, he hollered at me. Anybody around him got that. But I didn't let it worry me. I let it go in one ear and out the other. It was either that or go away and not come back, take your choice, and I needed the work. I thought he was sort of sweet."

In time, Claudia would change Harland Sanders' life, but neither had any inkling of that fact at that moment. She and Nell had apparently arrived just in time. Depression or not, business was growing fast, the six tables were not enough, and Harland was often forced to watch in anguish while customers left rather than face a long wait. It was like watching money walk out the door, and he couldn't stand it. He took what money he had and began to double the size of Sanders Cafe.

"I went down to North Carolina and bought these poplar boards," he said. "You don't see wood like that any more— forty-nine inches wide and the clearest, prettiest poplar you ever saw—and made booths out of them. People took to them right off. Gave them a feeling of privacy, don't you see?"

By trial and error, Harland was learning the restaurant business, and the more he learned the more he thought that there should be an organization of restaurant men, an association through which they could keep in touch, discuss ideas, new methods, problems, ways to increase quality and profit, ways to persuade people to eat out more. Some of this was Harland the restaurateur, some of it just plain Harland the booster, the joiner. "If Sanders couldn't find something to join," said Corbin businessman Robert Blair, "he'd start one himself."

This time he didn't have to start one. Late one afternoon, just as the dinner trade was beginning to filter in, a man approached him and introduced himself as a representative of the National Restaurant Association. "You've got a nice place here," he said. "I hear about you all over the area. But the Association could help you." He didn't need to continue with his spiel. Harland was an eager recruit. After they had talked a while, Harland asked him if there was an initial fee.

"Oh," said the man, "there's a membership fee, but it's only twenty-five dollars."

It is hard to believe that, at this point in his career, Harland did not have twenty-five dollars on hand. He still had his filling station, which was showing a profit, though it was small because he now had to hire men to run it. The restaurant was booming. He often had more customers than he could serve. He was meeting a sizable payroll—a cook, four waitresses, and usually a maintenance man. He had enough money in the cash register for the night's trade. Yet he later insisted that he did not at the time have the twenty-five dollars to join.

"Well, I just told this fellow, I said, 'Here, sit down and have a good meal on me, and then we'll talk business.' And I made him wait around until the dinner trade was gone and by that time I had the money."

At any rate, he joined. Soon he began getting Association literature and learned that there was to be a convention in Chicago that spring. Naturally, he had to go. Piling into his car, he and four other Corbin restaurant men drove to Chicago.

"We was all broke, you know, but that wasn't nothing in the Depression. We rented a single room, and we all slept in it. Took the mattress off the bed and three of us slept on that, with the other two sleeping on the springs. There was lots of food displays, there at the convention, and we ate at them free. I don't guess any of us spent over ten dollars, but we had a real time, I'll tell you."

Whether he benefited from the convention or not, the

Sanders Cafe continued to prosper, and the reason for it lay more in work and energy than in managerial ability. Harland was not a management genius. But he kept on top of everything, demanded that the place be kept spotless, and that service be quick and cheerful. And he watched the pennies.

Indeed, life would have been simpler and more comfortable had Harland been willing to settle down and devote himself solely to the restaurant. But ambition and the old restless energy drove him. For a while he became a district supervisor for the Works Progress Administration (a relief agency created under President Franklin D. Roosevelt to give temporary jobs to unemployed workers), checking on the activities of 120 men working in the Corbin area. In this job he became, of all unlikely things, a midwife, though he never explained where he got the knowledge or training to deliver babies. "Oh, I knowed a little about it," he once told the author, "enough to get the job done. All it takes is a little common sense. Hell, everybody knows where babies come from."

He got into this unusual career when one of the men he was supervising came to him in a panic, babbling that his wife was about to deliver and that he couldn't find a doctor. Harland tried to calm him, and assured him that he would take care of everything. Going to the man's house, which lay a horseback ride up a narrow hollow, he delivered the child, and when the news got around, he was asked to deliver others, partly, he suspected, because he didn't charge.

"That Sanders would do anything," remembers Lorene Hodge, of the Corbin chamber of commerce. "He would borrow Frank Mullins' old mule and go riding off some hollow to deliver a baby, just like he did it all the time."

On at least one occasion, he had the pleasure of having a child named after him, though on that occasion he had gotten a doctor to handle the delivery, as he did when there seemed to be difficulty.

It was also a joke around the Rotary Club that "Sanders delivered all those babies because he was afraid some of them were his," evidence of Harland's reputation of having a fondness for the ladies.

Harland was also beginning to dabble in politics. As a result of his part in getting a local man paroled, he was given a Kentucky colonel's commission by Governor Ruby Laffoon (and the next year turned around and supported Laffoon's political adversary, A. B. "Happy" Chandler, for governor). He was extremely proud of his colonelcy, and showed it around town until people got tired of hearing about it. Strangely, he didn't frame it, as most colonels do, and later lost it.

It was not, actually, a very big deal. While Kentucky colonel commissions are still prized, especially by non-Kentuckians, they can usually be obtained by anyone with a little political influence or a friend in the governor's office. Governors have traditionally used them to win friends, and have found that at times they have granted them, at the request of political friends, to people who were not exactly a credit to the custom. Lieutenant Governor Wilson Wyatt was once embarrassed to find that he had approved issuance of a commission to one April Flowers, who turned out to be a stripteaser in a northern Kentucky nightclub.

But though Harland was happy to be a Kentucky colonel, he made no effort to capitalize on his new rank. It was not until years later that he set out to become the Colonel.

His experiences in politics were not always happy ones. Happy Chandler, one of the more colorful politicians in a state that has produced many colorful ones, was making his first race for the governorship when his flamboyant tactics and courthouse oratory attracted Harland.

"Me and Tom Gallagher, Wade Chandler, and some others from Corbin worked for Happy," he recalled. "He had a speaking engagement down in Albany one day, when he found out that his sound truck had four flat tires. I went down—I was still running my filling station then—and put new tires on it and got it into Albany in time for the speech, and he came and thanked me. I rode around the county with Happy, introducing him to people, don't you see? We slept and ate together, just regular buddies. But after he got elected, he forgot who campaigned for him and took up with the professional politicians up in London. They got the plums. My friends didn't get anything."

He was thus soured on Chandler, who went on to become governor, U. S. senator, commissioner of baseball, and then governor for a second term. In the meantime, Harland had become friends with a personable young attorney from Lexington named John Young Brown, and backed him when he ran against Chandler's choice of a successor for governor. Brown lost, but he and Harland remained friends for the rest of Harland's life.

"I thought Happy oughta backed John Y.," he said, "because John Y. started out like a poor boy had to, the same as Happy and me." The Brown family often stopped at the Sanders Cafe on their way to Florida.

Using his political connections, such as they were, Harland lobbied harder than ever for improvement of US 25. The road was well-paved from Lexington to Corbin, but was little more than gravel from there to the Tennessee line. He led delegations to the state capital in Frankfort, seeking its improvement. He also worked for the upgrading of other roads in the area, gaining approval from civic and business groups. This persuaded him to enter the political arena himself, and he announced his candidacy for the state senate. He received a rude awakening.

Throughout his life, Harland Sanders seemed to have a hard time determining to which party he belonged, insisting that "I'm for the man, not the party." This did nothing to endear him to party regulars, who got out the vote. Actually, he was a conservative who felt about as comfortable in one party as in the other. He was a devout believer in free enterprise, the essential goodness of work, and the right to freedom from government interference.

But he was a registered Democrat, largely because he felt that Franklin D. Roosevelt was "getting things going," and he

ran in a district that was heavily Republican. Though he campaigned energetically, and spent more on his campaign than he
could afford, he lost. He was bitterly disappointed.

"I figured they'd appreciate what I had done for the roads
and all, you see. But they didn't. Not enough. I decided right
then and there I'd never run again." And he didn't, though he
continued to take part in politics, sometimes with awkward
results.

The year 1935 dealt Harland a painful blow when his
mother died. Though she had often regretted her failure to
give Harland a better start in life and more of the things that a
boy wants, she had loved him with the love a woman feels for
her firstborn, and had been a constant influence in his life. He
had loved her in return, and in her last years had tried to make
up to her for the hard times she had known after Wilbert
Sanders died. He visited her regularly, though he admitted
that he did not write, as she constantly urged him to do. She
was buried alongside her first husband in the Mount Moriah
Cemetery, and Harland had a single stone placed over their
grave. There is no mention of the name Broaddus, and Harland never mentioned his mother's dour second husband.

In 1935, Harland also began to devote some of his seemingly endless energy to two other aspects of his life—the Christian church and his endless but unsuccessful battle against the
Demon Rum. It was a curious struggle. While he was operating his filling station in Nicholasville, it was rumored in town
that Harland did a little bootlegging on the side; this would
not have been unusual, for many businessmen did, and the
practice was hardly frowned upon in an era when a good
bootlegger was a friend indeed. There is one story that some of
the local wags, knowing that Harland had a gallon of moonshine stashed in the rear of his station, started a hot argument
with him out front, and that while he was thus engaged some
of the boys sneaked around back and stole it, chortling because
Harland could not complain of his loss. Later, newspapermen
swore that when they stayed in Sanders Court in Corbin after
World War II, when Corbin was still dry, they would be

visited promptly by the friendly neighborhood bootlegger if they complained loudly enough to Harland that they wanted a drink. Whatever the truth of these stories, Harland always insisted that he despised the stuff. There is plentiful evidence that he did, and that he never touched it himself.

Part of his dislike of liquor, no doubt, stemmed from the difficulties his brother Clarence had with the bottle, part from the fact that bootlegging violence in the North Corbin area gave the neighborhood a bad name. Whatever his reasons, he became an enthusiastic advocate of Alcoholics Anonymous and would take carloads of reforming drunks to AA meetings in Lexington. He never turned away a drunk who was trying to sober up and sometimes had as many as seven at one time drying out in rooms of his motel, free of charge. He could be, as some of his fellow citizens put it, "corset-tight and willing to fight you for a dime" in other matters, but he kept drunks for free until they sobered up, and then fed them until they were able to face reality again.

Nevertheless, he became friends with one bootlegger who did business just down the highway from the Sanders Cafe, and on one occasion saved the man from the long arm of the law. Overhearing agents of the Internal Revenue Service discuss how they were going to trap the bootlegger with marked money, Harland slipped out the back door, hurried to the man's house, and warned him of the plot. The bootlegger gave Harland all of his money except for some change, and when the agents arrived with a search warrant, they could find no trace of the incriminating bills that they had been told were given to him. Grateful, the bootlegger later sent Harland word that some local thugs, angry because he had been instrumental in preventing one of their number from getting a parole from prison, planned to dynamite his restaurant. Harland promptly sent them word that he knew of the plan, and told them he would blow their heads off if they tried it. Puzzled but impressed by his knowledge of their plan, the hoodlums called off the dynamiting, and one of them later confessed to him that

"We never could figure out how you knew what we was planning to do."

As a boy, Harland had had the virtues of Christian conduct and the Christian church drilled into him by his mother, who, he said, "was at the church door when they opened it" and did not take frivolity on Sunday. ("Lord," said Harland, "we couldn't even whistle on Sunday.") But as a young man, he fell from grace to the extent that he seldom if ever went to church. Now he began to make up for it, bustling to church on Sunday morning and helping with Sunday school activities.

"I remember this one time," recalls Roy Houser, of Corbin, "when a bunch of us were sitting in the basement of the church talking about something, and Sanders came bustling in, the way he always did, and said, 'Now, we've got this Sunday school class meeting in the next room here tonight, and I don't want any of you sonsofbitches using any of that loud goddam rough talk.'"

His interest in Sunday school classes was a reflection of his concern for children, a genuine concern that continued as long as he lived. It was this concern that prompted his generosity toward the Galilean Children's Home, an orphanage near Corbin that was home to more than eighty children, and run by a minister named Vogel. Brother Vogel, as he was called, ran a very spare operation, and often called on Harland for help. Harland gave it, once giving Vogel a hefty check which he knew was no good, and then borrowing the money to cover it. Once, while he was running a furniture store in Corbin, one of the many enterprises in which he persisted in investing, he donated his stock of mattresses to the home. On Sundays during the summer months, he would take two five-gallon ice cream freezers, the old hand-crank type, out to the home, let the children help him turn the crank until the ice cream was ready, and then watch while they ate their fill. And at Christmas he always closed the restaurant to the public but paid his waitresses a twenty-dollar bonus to stay and help serve the entire home enrollment what was undoubtedly the best meal they ate all year. This show of concern for unfortunate children undoubtedly sprang from his memories of his own childhood, when he had known so much loneliness in a harsh and demanding world. In later years, his generosity would be repeated in more substantial form.

The Galilean experience, however, had a macabre ending. One day two girls from the home knocked on the door of a Corbin minister and, though frightened and unsure, poured out a story that shocked the community. Brother Vogel, they said, had for years forced the older girls at the home to have sexual relations with him, threatening them with prison if they told anyone. Having nowhere else to go, and having almost no contact with outsiders to whom they might have turned for help, the girls submitted. Brother Vogel had enjoyed the services of a youthful harem.

Vogel vehemently denied the accusations, but was indicted on a variety of sex and child-abuse charges. The lurid details revealed at his trial kept the region in salacious gossip for months. He was found guilty and sentenced to prison, though still protesting his innocence. Many people in Corbin believed him, too, until several years later, his daughter, Gladys Vogel Depree, published a book alleging all that the girls had charged, and more.

Harland never again mentioned the episode.

6

Even in his most miserable moments, when he was making sixteen cents an hour driving spikes and unloading coal cars for pennies, Harland Sanders dreamed of making it big. He never quit believing that someday, somehow, he would find a way, that something good would happen. And so he could not be content simply to run a successful restaurant. If one business made money, two ought to make twice as much. Anyhow, Sanders Cafe was about as big, he decided, as it could get.

Considering the times and its location, it was quite a restaurant. It had a fine reputation through eastern Kentucky, eastern Tennessee, and southwestern Virginia. "Ate at that Sanders Cafe down in Corbin," people would say, coming home from central Kentucky. "Good place to eat, I'll tell you. Best place around." Students traveling to and from the University of Kentucky and other schools around Lexington and Richmond made it a stopping point at vacation time. The dining room would be crowded and noisy with college kids heading for home at Christmas and Thanksgiving, and Harland would get furious trying to keep them from singing or drinking from the bottles they smuggled under the tables.

The growing popularity persuaded Harland that he should expand, start a chain of restaurants. He rented a building in Cumberland, in Harlan County, and spent weeks getting it into operation. He bought out an operator in Richmond and began a third. This got him, once again, into trouble with the law. On September 15, 1937, Associated Press dispatches out of Richmond carried an account that showed that Harland was still as bullheaded as ever.

"H. D. Sanders, president of the Kentucky Restaurant Association (he had already talked and smiled his way to the top of his adopted organization), director of the National Restaurant Association, and tourist chairman of the eastern division of the Kentucky chamber of commerce, was in the Madison County jail here today," read the story, "charged with operating a restaurant without an inspector's certificate. Sanders was charged in quarterly court here in April and fined $25 and costs, but refused to pay the fine."

Again Harland's sense of justice had been outraged. The previous owner, he pointed out to the court, had already paid the fee for the certificate for 1937; there was no reason why he should have to pay again. The judge pointed out in return that the previous owner was no longer in charge of the restaurant, that it had changed hands, and that the premises as operated by the new owner would have to be reinspected and recertified. Harland disagreed. He'd go to jail first, he declared. The judge accommodated him, and sentenced him to two weeks in jail. Harland asked that his incarceration be postponed until the following Monday, so that he could go home and straighten up some business matters. The judge, shaking his head, complied with the request, and on Monday Harland marched into court, surrendered, and marched off to jail.

To him, it was once more a matter of justice. Actually, it was, as the judge said wearily, childish. Harland had better things to do than sit in the Madison County jail. He finally realized it and, after eating the "awful goddam slop" he was fed, he gave up, paid for the inspection card (the judge agreed to waive the fine), and went back to work.

It was much ado about very little. Neither of his new restaurants proved successful, and he soon sold both of them. The failures were not too surprising. Harland County, where Cumberland sat at the end of a long, bad road, twenty-five miles from the county seat, had been shattered by the Depression. The coal market was going from bad to worse, coal prices were down, and as coal operators continued to lay off men and cut wages, the miners went out on a series of bitter strikes that sparked a decade of labor-management warfare. Hungry miners looted stores and begged food for their families. The Red Cross and church organizations shipped in carloads of food that only touched the spreading need. There were not enough people in Cumberland who could afford to eat in a first-class restaurant.

Harland had made another miscalculation in choosing Richmond as the site of his other venture. His location was not on the main traffic route, and he thus missed the trade that kept his Corbin cafe booming. People who could afford to eat out were in the habit of driving to nearby Lexington. And the students at Richmond's Eastern State Teachers College (now Eastern Kentucky University) could barely afford to eat in the dormitories. Harland had to hire too many people for too little trade. More important, he could not be there all the time to ride herd on the help.

None of this discouraged him. In the spring of 1937, he had had another idea. He had decided to go into the motel business. (It was not known as the motel business then, for motor hotels, from which the word motel was taken, were called either tourist courts or tourist homes.)

It was not an illogical decision. People forget (indeed, most Americans are too young to remember) how primitive most of the roadside hostelries were during the Depression years.

The average tourist court was a plain affair consisting of a row of cottages or cabins (some imaginative enterprisers built theirs in the form of Indian wigwams or Eskimo igloos), each containing a large bedroom and a basic bathroom. They were handy, and they were cheap, usually costing $1.00 or $2.00 a night for a single or a family. But they offered no air conditioning in the summer, and next to no heat in the winter. Screens seldom kept out the mosquitoes, the water often had a strong, sulfuric taste and smell, and it was a lucky family that got clean sheets and towels.

The court was usually run by a man and wife, one of whom would come out of the house, show you where to park, and guide you to the assigned cottage, asking where "you folks" were from, where you were going, and how you had found the roads up the way. There was no lobby, no bar, no restaurant, no pool, no playground. If you asked the next morning where you could get breakfast, you would likely be directed to a restaurant run by a relative of the court operator, a chummy place where the food was long on calories and short on vitamins, and run by a smiling lady who asked where "you folks" were from. (There was one saving grace, however; you could usually feed a family of four for about $2.85.)

Tourist homes were somewhat different. They could be fairly luxurious, though they often were not. In the South, especially, these were sometimes the residences of families who had seen better times, had been caught by the Depression, and had been forced to take in tourists for the night. In such homes, the rooms were attractive and comfortable, though the bath was usually shared by all, and there was little privacy. But the traveler more often found himself in the back room of a bungalow that smelled of oilcloth and kerosene stoves.

Harland had already proved to himself that he could operate a superior restaurant. In 1936, the famed Duncan Hines had stopped at the Sanders Cafe, and was so pleased with the fare that he listed the restaurant in his popular *Adventures in Good Eating*. This not only flattered Harland's ego, but, as he said,

"It sure didn't hurt business none, I can tell you." He never failed to mention it in his advertising.

He concluded that if he could develop a superior restaurant, it would be a snap to build a tourist court of equal caliber. He set about designing an L-shaped court of seven rooms, later expanded to seventeen, on the vacant lot adjoining his restaurant. Being Harland Sanders, a man with a close eye on the dollar, he couldn't just go down to the bank, borrow the money, hire a contractor, and build the thing. He bought the lumber from a friend, bargained with the man who sold him his gasoline for the brick (paying him an extra penny on each gallon of gasoline until the debt was liquidated), and then borrowed $5,500 from his friend J. D. Lee for furnishings. Actually this was an investment by Lee. He received for his loan a percentage of the business, which proved very profitable.

For very little of his own money, but a great deal of his own sweat, Harland soon had a modern motel, a row of rooms under a common roof, but with soundproofing built into the walls that allowed considerable privacy. The rooms were well, if plainly, furnished. He kept them immaculate. And he charged $2.50 per night per room, rather than the $1.00 or $2.00. He adopted strict rules about customers, although he later admitted that he could not always enforce them. Some say he did not try.

"I wouldn't take anyone living within a hundred miles," he declared righteously. "Most of the places along the road were nothing but hot-mattress joints, don't you see, rent a room two, three times a day and half the time never change a sheet. I wasn't going for mine to be like that. Wasn't going to have people go to the country club, get liquored up, and take a notion to sleep with somebody else's husband. Get a reputation like that and nice people, family people, won't stay with you."

Harland changed his sign to read SANDERS COURT instead of SANDERS CAFE. The motel was a money-maker from the day the first customer carried his bags in. It was such a good money-maker, in fact, that when he rebuilt it after a costly fire, Harland considered giving up the restaurant and enlarging the motel. That, he snarled, would free him from his endless hassles with cooks and waitresses, and the nerve-racking chore of finding, training, and supervising them.

The cooks, to hear him tell it, were invariably no-good sonsofbitches. The waitresses were stupid and incompetent. None of them knew how to run a kitchen or dining room, and at least once a week Harland would have a bellowing, cursing fight. According to some of his waitresses, he browbeat every cook but one; he could never, it seems, win an argument with her, and it would make him so mad that he would go over to the motel, get on the phone and give her unshirted hell and hang up before she could reply.

On the other hand, he figured, it would take no more than one or two maids and a maintenance man to run a good-sized motel. Actually, it is unlikely that he ever seriously considered closing the restaurant. It was probably nothing more than a way to let off steam after a fight with the help. At any rate, he never closed it. Instead, he expanded it to its final capacity of 142 seats.

"When I thought about it," he said, "I figured I could sleep a guy once a day, and I didn't get much more for sleeping a couple than for one. But I could feed a man three times a day and serve a couple six meals. Anyhow," he added modestly, "when I mentioned I might close it, everybody had a fit. Wouldn't hear of it."

But not even the new Sanders Court was enough to keep Harland happily occupied. He was still looking for a way to the big money, though he chose some rather strange routes. For example, at a time when few homes were being built and few people had enough money to spend on furnishings, he bought a furniture store (from which he gave the mattresses to the ill-fated Galilean Home; such charity may have contributed to the store's lukewarm profits. He later sold it). He also opened a plumbing shop—why, he never explained, except to say that "It looked like they could use one." He sold that, too.

Such restless enterprise was probably more than the mere pursuit of the dollar. He really wanted prominence more than profit. When, in 1948, Governor Earle Clements and the state chamber of commerce began the governor's tour, in which groups of city businessmen toured the smaller towns of the state, ostensibly to discuss mutual problems, Harland became an enthusiastic member of the tour.

The tour was far from pure business. At each town, the touring businessmen, usually including several state officials, would be met and entertained by the local civic and business clubs. There was some mild drinking (sometimes not so mild) and a great deal of male storytelling and adult horseplay on the bus. It was the kind of thing Harland loved. He was very proud when the tour stopped at Sanders Court, and he is said not only to have fed the bunch but to have shown them how to make a proper mint julep, strange conduct for an old bottle-battler.

No doubt all of this cost him money, but this was not a major consideration. He always gave away more than he could afford, whether to make a big show for his fellow citizens or through the impulses of genuine charity. Almost anyone who could muster a convincing hard-luck story could get a handout at the cafe, and in those Depression times most people had a well-polished hard-luck story. He had no use for bums, but if a man showed any willingness to work, he was never turned away hungry, and many of the jobs they were given were plainly make-work to justify the handout. A lot of profit from the restaurant went out the back door.

Harland liked to travel. He liked to drive to Florida, liked to pull up to a filling station in his big white Cadillac and say to the admiring attendant, "Fill 'er up," remembering the days when he was the attendant looking with envious eyes at owners of big Cadillacs. He made a point of stopping at restaurants in the bigger towns—Knoxville, Lexington, Atlanta—to see what they were doing and how their establishments compared with his. During these tours, he often drove through

Asheville, North Carolina, and in the spring of 1939 spotted what his promoter's eye told him would be a good spot for another Sanders Court. He plunged in, and late that year opened his second motel and restaurant.

It is significant that, after he got the new court running, he sent Claudia down to run it. This was an indication of more than his regard for her managerial ability. The fact is that there was already developing a strong bond between them.

She had long since become his top waitress. She had shown an ability to meet the public, handle the cash register, oversee the help, and take care of the court during Harland's numerous absences. Many nights, she had sat with him going over receipts, checking buying lists, and discussing menus. He bragged to others about her "good business head." He felt that she understood what he was talking about. And she was one person who was neither intimidated nor upset by his temper and language.

But the Asheville court never showed the return marked up by the original in Corbin, partly because it faced more serious-quality competition. He frequently went down to check on things, sometimes spending several days. During one of these trips, the first year the court was in operation, he received a frantic telephone call from one of his waitresses in Corbin. The motel, she told him, was on fire. It is difficult to believe that he received so calmly news that his chief investment was in flames, but according to his own account, he got the fire chief on the phone and coolly told him how to go about putting out the fire.

"I told them to go down a couple of rooms from the last one on fire and chop through a room, chop it down, walls, roof, everything. That way they could stop the spread of the fire and save the rest of the rooms. And that's what they did, and we saved seven of the seventeen rooms."

Then he rushed home. Incredibly, he had only $5,000 worth of fire insurance on the whole place, and had to borrow to rebuild. It was then that he considered—or said that he considered—discontinuing the restaurant. But he ended up making it bigger. The new motel was filled to capacity from the day he opened it.

In the meantime, a far more important event had occurred, although it did not seem significant at the time. One day, as he was walking across Main Street in Corbin, a hardware merchant called to him.

"Hey, Sanders," he said. "Come over here. I got something I want to show you."

"What is it?" asked Harland.

"This," the hardware dealer said, holding up a wooden-handled pot with what looked like a steam escape valve on top.

"What's that contraption?" Harland asked him.

"A pressure cooker," the man told him. It was one of the first Presto cookers (it is now on display in a glass case at the Sanders Museum in Louisville). "How do you cook your green beans?"

"Same as anybody," Harland replied. "Soak 'em overnight, put in side meat in the morning, and cook 'em, flavor 'em. Why?"

"Put them in this cooker with your meat, cover them with water, and cook 'em ten minutes. As good as if you cooked 'em all morning, and you can have stove-fresh green beans when you want 'em, without all the trouble. You can fix other vegetables, too."

Harland regarded the newfangled pot with suspicion, unwilling to believe that anything that easy could be any good.

"Take it and try it," the man told him. "And if you don't like it, bring it back."

"Well, I can't lose nothing," Harland admitted, and took the cooker back to the restaurant. Marching into the kitchen, he told the cook to string him some beans. He filled the pot up to the prescribed level with water, and when it was boiling, he put in the beans and a small square of lean bacon, added some selected spices, and clamped on the lid. Ten minutes later, he took off the pressure gauge, put the pot under cold water and loosened it, took out the beans, and told the cook to try some with him.

"I'll be durned," the cook said. They were good. Even Harland had to admit it. That afternoon he cooked some carrots and some cabbage. The next day he went back to the hardware store.

"That pressure cooker ain't bad," he conceded. "I guess I'll keep it for the time. Might as well get a couple more while I'm here."

He began to spend hours in the kitchen experimenting, to the disgust of the cook, whose job of getting out food was being complicated by having Harland taking up one or more of the burners. He overcooked some corn, which came out a mush, tried until he got it right, experimented with cooking tomatoes and green beans with the corn, and found that with proper timing it would cook just about any vegetable, or any meat that had to be boiled. It was just a matter of time until he got the idea to try the thing on chicken.

It was a flop. He was keenly disappointed, for he had a problem with fried chicken that he had never solved with conventional methods. If he prepared it ahead of time, he often had a lot left over, which amounted to a costly waste, since there was no way of telling how much fried chicken people would order on any given day. On the other hand, if he waited for customers to order before putting it on the stove, it took too long and the customer got restless. A hungry man, he knew, was apt to be short on patience, and if he was kept waiting too long, not even good food would restore his disposition. Harland tried deep frying chicken, like french fries, but while that speeded up the cooking time a little, the chicken often came out either soggy or crusty, and he was reluctant to serve it. He swore he would find a way.

"That pressure cooker of yours ain't worth a damn when it comes to fried chicken," he told his hardware merchant friend, who replied that he hadn't sold it as a frying pan.

"Well, by God, if it's a pressure cooker, it ought to pressure cook," Harland sulked. "I gotta find some way to fix chicken. That thing meant to take cooking oil?"

"Well, yes," the man replied, "but you'd better look in the manual."

Harland did, but his efforts were not successful. A Corbin friend, Eula Gordon, had given him a recipe for fried chicken, and he began experimenting with that, too, adding a spice, discarding it, adding another, changing proportions. He finally settled on a recipe and decided it was about as good as he had ever tested. Customers commented on it, too. A man from Michigan stopped in late one summer afternoon and ate some. Six months later, he returned and said, "I want some more of that chicken. That's the best I ever ate." Harland wasn't completely satisfied with it himself, but he felt he had a good thing going. But he couldn't seem to find the best way to cook it in a pressure cooker.

Other things took his mind off this particular problem. In 1940 he turned fifty, and the birthday, he confided to friends, jolted him. He had not achieved what he had hoped to achieve by that age. He felt time slipping away from him.

"Sanders didn't just daydream like other men," John Y. Brown, Sr., said later. "His dreams ate him up. He wanted to be a big man, looked up to." And though he was a local success, he felt that it hadn't happened.

Harland's self-esteem apparently needed frequent reinforcement, which is strange. He certainly could not consider himself a failure. He had started with nothing and had achieved a comfortable life-style, far better than most men in that time of depression. He was able to take care of his family and extend charity to others. He had a sound reputation in his business, and some influence in his hometown, though some people thought he was "a lot of show," "always putting on a big front," "hopping from one thing to another too much."

"Sanders was more of a promoter, a salesman, than he was a businessman," recalls Roy Houser. "He would always bluster in

with some big plan, some scheme. But he had a real persuasive
way about him. He could walk into a meeting that was just
torn apart with argument, and in five minutes he'd have everybody going along with him."

But he was never content. By 1941, he had enough capital
saved to try another venture. With World War II approaching,
the government had begun building a huge and mysterious
plant at Oak Ridge, Tennessee, a few miles northwest of Knoxville. Thousands of construction workers labored to build a
complex of buildings whose purpose no one knew and no one
was allowed to learn. Everybody knew it was something big
because it was so hush-hush. Trainloads of some kind of ore
rolled in, but nothing seemed to roll out. Thousands of workers
streamed in and out of the big buildings each day, and overnight a big town sprang up to accommodate them.

It was, of course, the Manhattan Project's diffusion plant,
where the first atomic bomb was produced. But for Harland, it
became simply a place where people had to eat. The government had set up huge cafeterias to feed the thousands of construction and factory workers, and Harland, chiefly because
of the reputation he had gained from his Corbin restaurant,
had been approached about running one of them. It sounded
like a good idea. It wasn't. In less than a year, he had quit.

"They didn't care what they fed them at that place," he
snorted. "And those people didn't care what they ate. I didn't
want anything to do with any damn place that just threw it out
there at them."

After Pearl Harbor, people who catered to the armed forces,
or produced materials for the mushrooming war industries,
could and did make fortunes. But Harland was not in a business
tailored to wartime restrictions. Gasoline and tire rationing cut
travel. Rationing of meat, sugar, and other scarce foods cut
into his menus. The draft took many of the salesmen who
had been his steady customers, and others, with nothing to sell,
took jobs in war plants.

Harland, in the meantime, had hired Ona May Leddington,

the daughter of his old adversary Matt Stewart, who had since married H. F. Leddington, one of Claudia's brothers. Ona May was no ordinary waitress. She demonstrated quickly that she could run the court about as well as Harland, and without the temper fits. With the war approaching, Harland turned the management of the place over to her and set about taking care of his other interests. Ona May managed the restaurant throughout the war and for several years afterward.

Harland's family life seems to have hit rock bottom during these years. Josephine, who lived much of the time in a room in the motel after Margaret and Mildred left home, blamed Claudia and other women for wrecking her marriage, but friends agreed that there was little marriage left to wreck. And Harland seldom had a placid relationship with his daughters. Margaret, especially, was spirited, strong-willed, and as stubborn as her father, and they clashed frequently. After the Colonel's death, Jim Sanders, his nephew, recalled one of the incidents.

"I remember one day down in Corbin, Unc said to me, 'Jim, come take a ride with me,' and we got in his car and he pulled out this letter he had in his pocket. He said it was from Margaret, and he started crying. Just sat there crying, and he said, 'Those girls going to kill me.'"

Claudia attributes the girls' attitudes, and Margaret's reputation in Corbin as a "wild one," to Josephine's influence.

"The way their mother brought them up, I don't think they had any love or respect for either mother or father," she said recently. "Naturally, they say now that they loved him, but that's now. I don't think either of them had any love or respect for their father. She brought them up not to have."

Caught in the tension between unloving parents, the girls could hardly have had an easy time. Josephine was a withdrawn woman, seldom affectionate, not the type to elicit confidences. Harland alternately gushed and raged, and tried to enforce a puritanical discipline for which he was hardly an example. At one point, he forbade Margaret to pursue her interest in sculpture ("playing with mud," he called it) and expressed rather unfatherly relief when, shortly before the war, she married James Adams in the first of her five marriages.

Meanwhile, Harland's business ventures weren't going very well, either. Rationing and wartime restrictions finally forced Harland to close the Asheville court.

"It wasn't only rationing," Claudia said later. "That was a good motel, and a good restaurant. We had about fifty rooms, as I recall. But Asheville was a seasonal town. It still is. People, tourists, go there in the summer, but you don't get any winter trade. A lot of people who have businesses in Asheville close them in the winter and run a second business down South, in Florida. It got so we just didn't have any trade to speak of.

"So in 1942, November 1942, I believe, H.D. [she often called Harland H.D.] drove me and my sister Joyce, and Marie Moore—a girl from Corbin, worked in a restaurant, too—out to Seattle, where we had jobs in Clark's Restaurant. Things just weren't good in Corbin during the war, but there was a lot of war industry in Seattle, and places like Clark's had a hard time finding good help. H.D. knew Mr. Clark; we'd met him at one of the conventions of the National Restaurant Association they held each May in Chicago, so we went out there in November, and came back the following August. I came back to my dad and mother's home in North Corbin, but after a while I went to live in Lexington."

With the end of the war, business boomed, and once again Harland saw a chance to ride the tide. The GI Bill had been passed by Congress to help returning veterans acquire or regain skills and become part of the nation's economic life, and Harland saw an opportunity in it. Renting a small warehouse, he hired the top bricklayer in Corbin, and opened a school to teach veterans bricklaying. It enrolled as many as 120 vets, some of whom went on to become successful in the building trades, but the economy rebounded much more vigorously than most economists predicted, absorbing the veterans into peacetime jobs. The bricklaying school was short-lived.

Like many others, Harland believed that the huge aircraft factories built for wartime plane production would soon be turning out planes as numerous, cheap, and popular as cars, and grabbed at the chance to get in on the ground floor. He leased some flat land at nearby London, bought nine Piper Cubs and one Piper Cruiser, and hired instructors to train veterans who wanted to become pilots. But two plane crashes in the London area (not his planes) cooled both his enthusiasm and that of veterans. He finally sold the field and planes at a $38,000 loss.

But Harland was not spending all of his time on new ventures. He still spent a lot of time in the kitchen experimenting with his pressure cookers. In the cookers, he felt, somehow lay the solution to his fried chicken problem. He was still trying changes in his chicken recipe, adding a spice here, putting in less of a spice another time. He knew that his chicken tasted good. But what he still sought was a way to quick-cook it so that he could prepare it as fast as it was ordered and serve it hot. He had found that the pressure cooker could be used for frying as well as boiling, but he had not found the correct recipe for cooking oil—the right temperature, the right procedure. It made the chicken either hard on the outside or soggy on the inside. He kept trying.

Margaret came home with her four-year-old son, Harland Adams, and Harland reveled in the role of grandpa. He took the boy with him everywhere, gave him the run of the restaurant (as long as he didn't annoy the paying customers), took him riding in the Cadillac, and bought him a pony. When little Harland wanted to ride, they simply removed the back seat of the Cadillac and let the pony ride there, his head sticking out the window, out to the country. Some people thought it strange to see a pony riding in a Cadillac, but others just shrugged it off as another Sanders eccentricity.

In 1947, to the surprise of no one, Harland and Josephine were divorced. There was no reason to continue the marriage. It had been a formality for years. His life was with Claudia.

"I liked both Josephine and Claudia," Ona May (by that time, Ona May Barbati) said years later, "but that just wasn't a marriage. He was a very emotional man, easily touched. Anything could bring tears to his eyes, and he needed somebody who could appreciate that. And Josephine just didn't care for sex. That's all. Sex is a normal drive in life. It was with him. But not with her."

Harland declared that he always thought that marriage was supposed to be forever, that he disapproved of divorce, and after his divorce never intended to marry again. This was almost surely untrue. There is every evidence that he had wanted to marry Claudia for some time, and in 1949 he did. And it was probably the best thing that ever happened to him. Claudia was exactly what he wanted and needed. She understood him, was accustomed to his bluster and sudden outbursts of temper. She could deal with him without losing her composure. And she was someone he could talk with about his dreams and plans.

Nineteen forty-nine brought another event, seemingly insignificant at the time, that was to have a part in redirecting Harland's life. Lieutenant Governor Lawrence Wetherby, with whom Harland had become acquainted on the governor's tour, presented Harland with another Kentucky colonel's commission. He didn't lose this one. He kept it and framed it.

Before, he had been just Harland Sanders. Now, he began to think of himself as Colonel Sanders. And Colonel Sanders would be, in subtle and then major ways, a person different from Harland. He would be able to do things Harland had wanted to do but had never done, be things Harland had never been. In time, Harland would become submerged in the identity of the Colonel.

7

All life is change. For some, the change is sudden and dramatic—crushing failure, promotion to power. The drunk quits drinking; the sinner gets religion. But for most, change comes slowly and is beyond the power of each person to resist. Hair turns gray. The face sags. One morning you notice that the skin on the backs of your hands is loose and freckled. Knees and shoulders creak.

But for Harland Sanders, the great change in his life was chosen, self-imposed, and while it did not happen overnight, or like Paul's blinding light on the road to Damascus, once begun it became irreversible, changing the man and his personality, his life. He could not himself pinpoint the time when he first had the idea to become Colonel Sanders, but it undoubtedly had its origins with the second Kentucky colonel's commission he received in 1949. He began referring to himself as Colonel Harland Sanders. He signed his name Colonel Harland Sanders. His hair was turning white, and he began to let it grow rather full, whereas he had always kept it short and clipped high on his head. He grew a mustache and finally, as though to complete the image, a short goatee.

"Nobody took it seriously at first," says Corbin's Robert Blair. "At first, we thought he was just joking, and then when he kept on, we figured it was another one of his gimmicks, a way to advertise. We used to ask him when he was going to change the name of his place to Colonel Sanders Court, sell Colonel Sanders' fried chicken. Finally, I think everybody just sort of accepted it; if Harland wanted to be a colonel, all right, we'd go along with it."

One day while Harland was having his hair cut, his barber suggested that he ought to "go whole hog" and get himself a white suit and string tie like the old Kentucky colonel in the cartoons. Actually, Harland had already considered doing just that, but the suggestion triggered action. He had a white linen suit tailored, and fashioned a string tie from some grosgrain ribbon. People began calling him "Colonel," jokingly at first and then as a matter of course.

But the outward transformation was not quite complete. Before it turned gray, Harland's hair had a reddish tinge, and while his hair and mustache turned an appropriate white, his goatee refused to follow suit, keeping its reddish tinge. Then one day, about the time he was beginning his effort to franchise his fried chicken recipe, he stopped by the chamber of commerce, where Lorene Hodge had volunteered to type his letters to potential customers.

"It wasn't any big thing on my part," she said. "He didn't have more than a half-dozen a month. Not worth hiring a secretary for, and I didn't mind typing them. Anyhow, one day he came barging in the way he did—Sanders couldn't come into a place without you thinking he was going to make some big announcement—and someone, I forget who, said to him, 'Colonel, you ought to do something about that beard of yours, get it bleached to match your hair.' He got sort of red, and grinned and said that he'd tried to, that his barber had washed it with Clorox, but it turned orange, and he had a time getting it out. So I said to him, 'Why don't you go over to Lorayne's and get her to do it?' Lorayne Campbell ran the beauty shop across the street from our old office, Lo's Beauty Shop, and that's where Claudia always had her hair done, and I told him I'd call her and she would bleach it for him. And he did. Went right over to the beauty parlor and Lorayne bleached it for him.

"To tell the truth, I was surprised that he did it, going to the beauty shop. You know how he was. He put on a big show, but he was really pretty touchy. But he did, and Lorayne did a good job for him. He seemed real pleased with it, and any time it started growing out, he'd go back and she'd bleach it out again, until it turned naturally white. That was after he started wearing the white suit and black tie all the time. And I mean all the time. Winter as well as summer. He had a special heavy material made into a suit for winter. Now, this was before he started selling franchises, the time he got his beard dyed. About 1950. He didn't start selling franchises until a few years after that, as I recall. I guess it was then I started doing his letters."

Harland may not have been franchising in 1950, but he was giving a lot of time and thought to fried chicken. He had just about settled on a cooking method. He had no technical knowledge of engineering, knew nothing about thermodynamics, the properties of heat, the factors of heat retention, or the relative conductivity of different materials. But he knew what he was trying to do: He had to find out how hot to get his cooking oil, whether to prefry his chicken in order to seal in the flavor, and how long to cook it under pressure to make it tender without making it soggy. Then he had to find out how long and at what heat he should keep it in the warming oven before it lost its warmth and consistency.

By persistent trial and error, he had solved most of the problem. He concluded that he had to prefry it only a matter of seconds before applying the pressure (he later abandoned the prefrying altogether). He then cooked it seven minutes under fifteen pounds of pressure, with his cooking oil at 250 degrees to produce the taste and texture he wanted. He learned that a warming oven at 160 degrees kept the chicken hot for at least five hours without drying it out (a process not now used), making it possible to serve for dinner any chicken left from lunch. And he settled on a cooking oil that fitted the process, although he could not figure out how to clean the oil for reuse, making it a very big cost factor. Oil used more than three times tended to get carbon-laden and turned the chicken an unattractive color. The chicken fat, which fried out during the cooking process, also discolored the chicken.

He faced two other big problems. The biggest pressure cookers he could find would handle no more than two chickens at one time. He solved this, in a manner of speaking, by using several cookers. But even the largest range top would accommodate no more than half a dozen, and he needed several for preparing his vegetables.

And he was still not satisfied with his recipe. People raved about the chicken. It had already replaced country ham as the cornerstone of the restaurant's reputation. He liked it himself. But it seemed to him that something was missing. Then in 1952 he hit upon his "secret ingredient," the one thing that completed his "eleven herbs and spices."

There was nothing mysterious about Harland Sanders' recipe for frying chicken. Eula Gordon's recipe depended heavily on a commercial seasoning salt that contained herbs and spices; Harland's secret lay in the herbs and spices he added. His procedure was the simple one followed in most American homes: dip the piece of chicken in a "wash" (Harland pronounced it "warsh") of eggs and milk ("They gotta be fresh," he would bellow at his cooks. "Good fresh eggs and whole fresh milk"), then roll it in flour to which the herbs and spices had been mixed. The flour was not ordinary flour. An acceptable flour could be bought commercially, but Harland insisted that his specially mixed flour provided a tastier crust. And the proportion of herbs and spices to be mixed with the flour, while not secret, was important.

"One day this fellow named Noe, owned a big boat dock down on Lake Cumberland, what they call a marina nowadays, came to see me," Harland recalled. "He was bringing this big crowd of people up the river to see his outfit, don't you see, and he wanted something handy and good to feed them. He ordered five hundred fried chicken box lunches, biggest order I'd ever had. Well, sir, it just came to me that maybe this was the time to try this one ingredient I'd been thinking about. It would give me a chance to try it out on a lot of people at one time, you see, so I did. And when I ate that first piece and we started packing all those boxes, I knew that was it. It was just what I wanted." (Old-timers in the company said that the magic ingredient was nothing more than confectioner's salt. Whatever it was, it did the trick.)

"I knew I was right when these people started coming in and telling me how good the chicken was," said Harland. "They couldn't say enough about it. I made a lot of customers out of that one order."

The secret recipe was set. But, actually, the success of Harland's fried chicken was due not so much to the kind of seasoning he used as to the fact that he used seasoning. As John Y. Brown, Jr., whose fortunes would become intertwined with those of Colonel Sanders, said later, "It was the idea of seasoning his chicken when he cooked it that was revolutionary, not the fact that he used so much of one spice and so much of another.

"Before the Colonel came along, the average restaurant just rolled chicken in flour and fried it; some would roll it in milk or milk and eggs first, then in flour and fry it, leaving it to the customer to season it to taste. But the average customer doesn't know how to season food to bring out its optimum flavor. Great chefs know this. You don't see them putting salt and pepper or a bottle of ketchup on the table in fine restaurants. They know which seasoning brings out the flavor and they add it when they cook. That's the difference between a fry cook and a great chef.

"And what a lot of people never really understood was that the Colonel was a great cook. He was an innovator. He knew how food was supposed to taste and he prepared it so that it tasted that way. So when his chicken came out of the kitchen, it not only tasted the way it should, it tasted better than anyone else, including the customer, could make it taste. And therein lay his real secret."

Business was good in 1952, and getting better, and Harland could afford to take time off to go to the annual convention of the National Restaurant Association in Chicago. That was fortunate, for at the convention he met Leon "Pete" Harman, the owner of a small restaurant, the Dew Drop Inn, in Salt Lake City. Pete Harman was thirty-two, the Colonel sixty-two, when they met. But since neither of them drank or smoked, they found themselves often thrown together and spent a lot of "hospitality" hours discussing business, food, preparation, menus, and the like. When the Colonel discovered that Harman was a Mormon, he tried to keep himself on good behavior and curb his profanity. He didn't know anything about Mormons, and was rather suspicious of them, but the two men, despite the differences in age and background, took to each other, and a friendship began that would last throughout the Colonel's life. The friendship was cemented when they met again at a restaurant short course, conducted by the Association, in Chicago, and again found themselves among the few nonsmokers and nondrinkers.

A few months later, Harland set out on one of those curious undertakings for which it is hard to find a logical explanation. A group of churchmen, including his Corbin minister, the Reverend John Chambers, decided to attend a conference of the Christian church in Sydney, Australia. Harland decided to go along, hoping, he said, that the experience would cure him of his cursing. Why a conference nearer home would not have sufficed, or why he chose not to take Claudia with him, remain a puzzle. In any event, he traveled to San Francisco with a group of Corbinites, where they met the larger group waiting to fly to Australia. Having some time to kill, they went to the airport to inspect the plane on which they were to fly, and were surprised to find a conventional, four-engine plane. "I thought it would be one of those flying boats," Harland said later, "like those big clippers that they flew across the ocean before the war."

"Tell me, Colonel," Reverend Chambers asked jokingly, "what happens if those engines quit?"

"I'll tell you what happens," Harland said. "All you preachers will go on to heaven, and leave me to swim home."

On the way to San Francisco, Harland stopped off in Salt Lake City to see his new friend Pete Harman, who asked him to dinner. Harland accepted, but asked that they eat at the restaurant, and that he be permitted to fix his Kentucky fried chicken for the Harman family. An hour before dinner, he went into the restaurant kitchen, rummaged around for the necessary ingredients, and prepared what he hoped would be a treat—fried chicken, mashed potatoes, crackling gravy, vegetables, and biscuits. He watched closely as the Harmans dug in, and was gratified to see that nothing was left. Harman confessed that the chicken was the best he had ever eaten, better than he served to his own customers, and praised the gravy. The Colonel was elated.

"Tell you what I'll do," he said. "Let me fix you up with some pressure cookers, and I'll show your cook how to fix chicken the way I do. And I'll sell you my secret recipe of herbs and spices so what you serve will taste just like what you just ate. We'll agree on the price you pay me. How does that strike you?"

He had already toyed with the idea of selling his recipe to other restaurants, but this was the first time he had tried to put his thoughts into concrete terms. How much should he charge for his herb-and-spice mixture? How could he be sure no one would duplicate it? Should he mix it with the flour he recommended and sell both? Should he just sell the cookers, the warmers, and the recipe for a flat sum, or should he try to charge by the amount of chicken the man served?

Of one thing, he was convinced—he had the secret for the

best-tasting chicken he had ever known. If he was going to sell it, he needed a name for it, and a way to keep anyone from cutting in on the name.

His big plans took a setback when Pete Harman wouldn't commit himself to buy the recipe. The Colonel thought that Pete would jump at the chance, especially after eating the chicken and gravy, but his young friend hedged. He'd think about it, he said, and the Colonel let it drop, not wanting to impose. He went on to Australia and what he hoped would be salvation from dirty talk.

He spent a lot of time on the trip thinking about his plan. What should he call his chicken? He ran through a list of possible descriptives—lip-smacking, crispy, juicy, down-home, kitchen-fresh, tooth-tender? How about Colonel Sanders' Fried Chicken? With his picture as the Kentucky colonel? Maybe he ought to bring in the name of Kentucky. How about Colonel Sanders' Kentucky Fried Chicken? Was that better than Southern Fried? Farm Fried? Home Fried? Yeah, he decided, it was. Kentucky had a good ring to it—rolling bluegrass meadows, white fences, pillared old mansions, smells of cooking wafting out of the old kitchen. And, after all, he *was* a genuine Kentucky colonel. Kentucky Colonel Fried Chicken? Kentucky Colonel Sanders' Fried Chicken? Nope. Colonel Sanders' Kentucky Fried Chicken. That would do it. He decided to incorporate as soon as he got home. Thought maybe he'd better copyright the name, too, and his picture, with the white suit, goatee, and all.

Upon his return, Claudia met him in San Francisco and they took a VistaDome train back to Chicago, stopping off in Salt Lake City to see Pete Harman.

("In Salt Lake," he told the author, "we caught a streetcar out to Pete's place—didn't have enough money for a cab, don't you see?" It was impossible to take this seriously. Though he did make and spend money recklessly, and was often broke or near-broke as a result, he was, at this point, a man who had a growing business, who had bought and sold a half-dozen others over the previous five years, who had just traveled halfway

around the world to a church conference, and who was now
riding a luxury train home.)

Maureen McGuire, later the Colonel's personal secretary,
said that he often twisted facts if the twist produced a better
story.

"Of course he had the money for a cab. But I'll have to say
this: If he didn't feel like giving the cabbie a big fare, he
probably would have gone on and ridden the streetcar. He just
didn't like to spend money, especially in little amounts. He'd
give away ten thousand dollars at lunch, and then do anything
not to pick up the check for the lunch. I don't think he had a
feel for money in big amounts, and when you got into the high
figures, it didn't mean much to him, because all of his life he
had been fighting for little money. But when you got down to
twenty dollars, he could understand that."

In any event, the visit was a great success. Pete and the
Colonel discussed the idea of marketing the Sanders chicken
recipe, and while the idea probably evolved from the general
discussion, many people think that it was Pete who first suggested that the Colonel franchise his cooking process and
charge each franchisee a few cents for each chicken sold. By
the time he got back to Corbin, he had his franchising plan
pretty well in mind.

"I knew I had a good idea," he later told the author, "but I
was beginning to see that it wasn't going to be easy, either. I
knew I couldn't give a franchise to just anybody with any old
greasy-spoon restaurant. A man that will let a dirty cook keep
a dirty kitchen won't take the trouble to fix a recipe right, and
I knew my chicken had to be cooked right, the way I told
them to cook it, if it was going to be as popular as it could be.

"And how was I going to check on how many chickens a
man sold using my recipe? Fact is, I couldn't. Now, I could tell
something about how he was doing by the amount of herbs
and spices he bought, don't you see. But in the long run it was
just going to be a matter of getting honest people. I figured if I
picked good people, a handshake would be all the contract I'd
need. Figured if a man was good enough to shake hands with,

I wouldn't have to be checking on him. If he wasn't, checking wouldn't do no good."

There was business to be looked after before he took off on any franchising venture, however. A third motel and restaurant, opened in Georgetown, Kentucky, the previous year, wasn't making money. It was the old story—good town, poor location, and no Colonel to run things. He looked for a way to unload it, so that he could concentrate on his franchising. He was sixty-three years old now, and there are indications that he was experiencing the feeling of urgency that often hits men who discover that their years are running out. According to people who worked for him during these years, he was becoming extremely crotchety, irritable, almost tyrannical toward his employees.

"Harland Sanders was a total Jekyll-and-Hyde in those days," says Norma Crawford, wife of Jim Lee Crawford, publisher of the Corbin *Times-Tribune*. "I was a student at Transylvania College then, and worked at his place during the summer. It was a nice place, the nicest around. Mothers didn't mind their daughters working there. Sanders kept it orderly. He was getting famous as the Kentucky Fried Chicken king—that was in 1952 and '53—but here in Corbin, we thought the Colonel thing was kind of silly. Actually, I suppose he was better known in other parts of the country than he was here in Corbin, as the Bible says about a prophet being without honor in his own land.

"I hated working there. Hated it. Sanders paid just what he had to and not a penny more, but the tips were good and I needed the money for college, so I stuck. He had a violent temper and a vile tongue, and he took the temper out on his help. If he was feeling bad, or if something went wrong with business, he took it out on the girls and the cook. Oh, he'd go into the dining room and just charm the customers out of their chairs, bowing and smiling, and then come back to the kitchen and curse the poor cook, throw a temper tantrum. He was just plain mean to the girls."

John Y. Brown, Jr., later claimed that Harland's temper tantrums were mostly staged to drive his employees to the perfect performance he demanded. If so, his performances were extremely realistic. On one occasion, he is reported to have hit the cook with a pot of gravy. On another, he is supposed to have thrown a knife, "almost as heavy as a cleaver," at the hapless chef. During his years at Corbin, only one cook was supposed to have stood up to him.

"I'll say this," says Norma Crawford. "He was a perfectionist. He demanded the best for his customers, and I mean *demanded*. If a piece of lettuce was too big, bigger than bite-size, he would have a fit. If a drop of dressing spilled on the side of the salad plate, he would have a fit. We served honey at every table, every meal, so the customers could have it with their biscuits, served it in a big pedestal bowl. After each customer, that bowl had to be taken out and the honey emptied into a fresh bowl. He didn't want any chance of a drip spot on the side of that bowl. Everything had to be just so. If there was a dirty place on the floor or a spot on a table or each setting wasn't just right, he raised Cain. It really made you nervous working there.

"He was a strange man in lots of ways. We went to the same church. He really liked church, and was generous with it. But toward the end of his stay in Corbin, he started coming in late to service, real late, sometimes just five or ten minutes before the sermon was over. He'd walk down the aisle in his white suit and sit right in the front row, looking all around as though he wanted to be sure he was seen, nodding his head to the sermon."

("I remember one time the Colonel gave the church a big coffee urn," recalled Yvonne Eaton, another member of the Corbin church and later a writer for the *Courier-Journal* in Louisville. "He brought it in just before church, so everyone could see it. He wanted everybody to know where it came from. Announced that he was giving it to the church so that the people wouldn't have to have their coffee at home and could get to church on time. And then he was late himself all the time.")

"Claudia—Mrs. Sanders—was very different," says Norma Crawford. "She was really very sweet, very ladylike. All the help liked her. She'd come over late in the afternoon, go out to the kitchen and get a little something to eat and talk to the girls, and then go out and take over the cash register. She never raised her voice. When he went into one of his cursing fits, she'd just say, 'Oh, Harland,' as if she were talking patiently to a silly child, and ignore him.

"The Colonel was a great cook, truly. I always thought he deserved credit for the ham biscuit. It was the first I ever ate, and it was certainly the best. He'd put a slice of ham in the biscuit and fold it over before cooking it, but he would also put little pieces, very small pieces, of ham in the dough, so the flavor went all through it. It was delicious. He had lots of little specialties like that. The only trouble was that he was a great cook, and when the plain cooks that he hired didn't do as well as he did, he raised the roof.

"And jealous! They had a big ceremony when they dedicated the new Christian church, and they expected him to make a good contribution—you had to say that for him, he was always generous with the church. But the women of the church fixed this big lunch, you know, and they bought their chicken from the supermarket. When he found that out, he just blew up. Said he wouldn't give them a penny, and you can imagine how he phrased it. I don't know whether he stayed mad or not. He usually didn't, but while he was mad, he was a holy terror."

Staged or genuine, these temper tantrums amazed, shocked, and often alienated people throughout the Colonel's life. The author, interviewing him for a profile, asked him, in the course of the interview, when he and Claudia were married. "In 1950," he replied. "No," said Claudia, "it was 1949." "Well, I guess I know when I was married," he bellowed, "and it was 1950." "I was married then, too," Claudia said quietly, "and it was 1949."

The author suggested that the marriage license would show the date, and Claudia went upstairs and shortly produced the document with its date. She had been right; it was 1949. The Colonel subsided.

But a few days later, he stormed into the newspaper office, brandishing his cane and threatening to whip the writer, who was fortunately out of the office.

"That sonofabitch wouldn't believe me, wouldn't take my word for it that we was married," he stormed to the editor, who stared at him as though he couldn't believe what he was seeing. "Made my wife go upstairs and show him our marriage license to prove we was married."

The editor, bemused at the sight of the white-suited fury shaking a big black cane at him, assured the Colonel that the writer had meant no affront, but was just trying to be accurate, and showed the Colonel a copy of the article, then in preparation. The Colonel read it, calmed down, and invited the editor and his wife to dinner. The relieved editor reported that the dinner was excellent, the Colonel a charming host.

In June 1953, the Colonel enjoyed what he considered a mystic stroke of fortune when he managed to unload the Georgetown motel and restaurant, and even made a small profit on the deal. The transaction did a lot to make him a believer in horoscopes. The year before, while at the NRA convention in Chicago, he had eaten at a restaurant where an astrologer offered to devise a horoscope for any diner who wished it. The Colonel said he would like one, though insisting later that he didn't "put any stock in that stuff." The horoscope woman told him that big things were about to happen; between June 28 and 30 of the next year, she declared, he would get a large sum of money. Not only that, but shortly afterward he would be offered an even larger sum.

Sure enough, on June 28, 1953, a man paid the Colonel $29,000 for his lease on the Georgetown motel and restaurant. Two days later, a man from Cynthiana, Kentucky, offered him $164,000 for Sanders Court. It shook the Colonel. A belief in astrology, he felt, was somehow un-Christian. But he couldn't get around the fact that the astrologer had hit it right on the nose. The incident left him with a lingering belief in horoscopes that would have a near-disastrous result.

The Colonel was tempted by the offer for Sanders Court, but turned it down. Business, he figured, was too good. If somebody was willing to pay $164,000 for his place, the place was obviously worth more. But no sooner had he turned down the offer than he began worrying that he had made a mistake; $164,000 was a lot of money—he could use it to finance his new venture. On the other hand, it would be good to have the court to fall back on if he was not able to franchise his Kentucky Fried Chicken, which he had incorporated. As might be expected, Pete Harman was his first franchisee, offering Kentucky Fried Chicken under an agreement that was nothing more than a handshake. The Colonel installed the pressure cookers for him, taught the cooks how to cook the chicken ("Dip it in the warsh and roll it in the flier"), and helped Pete with the opening-day promotion, appearing in his colonel suit, mingling among the guests, urging everyone to give Kentucky Fried Chicken a try. As he approached Harman's restaurant, a modest affair that Pete would soon exchange for a much larger one, he saw "the biggest sign you ever saw" advertising COLONEL SANDERS' KENTUCKY FRIED CHICKEN, highlighted by a likeness of the Colonel himself.

"It made me feel good," he said. "I said to myself, 'This is going to go.'"

In the winter of 1954, he began his first tentative attempts at franchising. He made a good start. Driving through Louisville, he stopped in Kaelin's Restaurant on Newburg Road to see his long-time friends, Carl and Margaret Kaelin, and to eat one of their famous cheeseburgers, which Kaelin's is credited with originating.

"My father-in-law, Carl Kaelin, and I operated the restaurant then," says current owner Herb Raque. "And Pappy—that's what I always called the Colonel—would drop in from time to time. We knew him from Corbin and conventions, and he was a good friend. When he told us he was franchising his chicken, we didn't think much of it, but we went along. He chose the places he wanted to put in his franchises by dropping in and eating there himself.

"We just shook hands on it. No contract. Later on, when I asked him for a contract, he didn't like it. 'Ain't an agreement with me enough?' he hollered. 'You think I'm not a gentleman?'

"He was a great companion. As far as I'm concerned, old Pappy was just fine. I traveled with him some when he was starting out. He drove that big old Cadillac. He was death on smoking. Didn't like liquor, but was death on smoking. One day we were driving up through Ohio, and I lit a cigarette, and the first thing I knew, every window in that thing was open. 'What are you doing?' I said, and he said, 'When you put out that goddam cigarette, I'll put up the goddam windows.'

"After he got the franchising going, we organized the first training kitchen here. Pappy and I set it up. He'd bring in the owners or their employees to learn how to do it. He didn't have too much control over them then, but later, when a franchise became so valuable, he could always threaten to cut them off, and most of them would shape up.

"I don't have a franchise any more, but I'm still frying chicken the way old Pappy showed me back then in '53 or '54, I forget. I think it was 1954. We bought his spices and sent him a nickel for each chicken we served. Honor system; that was it. Later on, KFC let you buy stock for the number of franchises you had. Money I made from that stock remodeled this place. Yessir, he was all right. You don't find them like him any more."

Selling (actually, giving away) the franchises was slow work, and the Colonel soon hired his sister Catherine's son, Lee Cummings, to help, and later made him president of Kentucky Fried Chicken. He was also having his usual problems with Sanders Court, for Ona May had quit and started her own place, Ona May's, in downtown Corbin.

"There were no differences between us," she says now. "Oh, we had our battles. Claudia said we were too much alike not to fight. But that wasn't it. I just wanted my own place. And I had a good place. But it didn't pay out too well. That was about the time the railroads were replacing coal-burning engines with diesels, and that cut the roundhouse there in Corbin. Thousands of people all of a sudden out of work. My place didn't really go over because of that, and that's the reason I sold out and went to Lexington and started the Colonel's. I owned fifty percent, the Colonel owned fifty, or forty-nine. I think he gave Mildred one percent. He really helped me financially. I always knew I could count on him. He sold out his interest to Joe Smiley in 1957, but I knew I could count on him anyhow."

Claudia didn't like to see Ona May leave. She liked her. "After we were married, H.D. always allowed Josephine and the girls to come to our house, but none of them spoke to us for a year after we were married. Then I guess they decided they needed a little money, and they came around—you'd of thought it was just one big family."

Harland was trying to find good salesmen. One of those he approached was Don Towles, now public affairs director for the Louisville *Courier-Journal*.

"I remember the last time we stopped there, not long before he sold out," says Towles, "and Harland was around the tables in that white suit. He stopped by the table where Johnny Whisman and I were sitting, and he said to us, 'Boys, tell you something. I'm getting ready to start franchising my Kentucky Fried Chicken. It's going to catch on like wildfire, boys, and I'd like to have you with me on it. Come to work for me, and we'll make a fortune.' Well, I didn't take him seriously. It was just old Harland, up to one of his wild schemes. We told him, 'No thanks,' and he said, 'All right, you're going to miss out.' By George, he was right."

The Colonel was on the road more than half the time now, and making a few sales. It wasn't easy.

"I guess they wondered who this old geezer was in a white suit, coming in and telling them how to cook chicken. Some of them wouldn't talk to me at all. Others said they didn't think chicken would ever be a big item on a menu."

He and Claudia got up a little act. They would go to a restaurant to which Harland had sold a franchise and, after he had showed the cooks how, the two of them would circulate among the guests, in costume, encouraging them to order some of that fine Kentucky Fried Chicken. The Colonel wore his colonel suit, and Claudia was decked out in an old-fashioned Southern belle costume, complete with hoop skirt and ruffles. Some people were pleased, some puzzled. But the two of them made an impression, which was the object. They made people remember that they had eaten not just any chicken, but Kentucky Fried Chicken. The Colonel was confident they would like it and order it again.

Claudia was not enthusiastic about her Scarlett O'Hara role, but she went through the paces.

"Putting on that hoop skirt and all, and him in his colonel suit, that wasn't my idea, I can tell you that," she says. "But I went along with it, and we went all over the country, from New York to Florida. I liked the traveling part.

"He was the main one, putting over the deals. It all depended on him, not me. I told him, 'It's up to you and how you act. You'll either go over or you'll go under, the public will make you or break you.' I was always around, but I didn't want him introducing me. I didn't see any need for them to know me, so I'd hear all the remarks people would make, you know, about him, not knowing who I was, and that was useful."

But while they were building up the franchise business on the road, misfortune was shaping up back home. Throughout his years in Corbin, Harland had worked tirelessly for better roads. When the new Interstate highway program was started in the early fifties, he was confident that the increased north-south traffic would prove a blessing for Sanders Court, since there was bound to be an interchange between the new I–75 and US 25, which ran past his restaurant. The prospect of Interstate tourists turning off at his sign was one of the reasons he turned down the offer for the court in 1953.

Then the plans were announced for the routing of I–75.

There would be an interchange with US 25, all right, but US 25 was going to be rebuilt and rerouted. It would no longer run past his court. Only local traffic would come past him. The golden tourist flow would miss him altogether.

It was cruel irony. The road improvement he had sought now threatened to ruin him. He and Claudia held long discussions about what they should do. He walked the floor, fuming. They decided to sell, if they could find a buyer. There was no use hanging their hopes on a motel and restaurant that would soon have no traffic to feed them.

There were no takers. He advertised. He waited. Finally, after months of frustration, he put the court up for public auction. It brought $75,000—furnishings, equipment, and all.

That and the small amounts trickling in from his franchises were all that he had in the world. And now he was sixty-five years old. He drew his first Social Security check. It was for $105. That, he had to face, was not going to carry them very far very well.

Once more he was down. But he was not out. He was Colonel Sanders. And he had his plan.

"The wonderful thing about the Colonel," John Y. Brown, Jr., said, "is that he never thought of quitting. When he got that first check, he sat down and, he told me later, said to himself, 'Now, by God, there's something in this world I can do better than anyone else, and the only thing I can think of is frying chicken, so that's what I'll do.' And that's when he really started pushing."

The Colonel decided that, to launch his franchise business, he needed a more central location. He and Claudia sold their home, paid off their debts, and bought a home in Shelbyville, Kentucky, a big rambling white-brick set on a tree-shaded lot on Louisville Road. He chose Shelbyville because, he said, "I needed to be near a big town, but I didn't want to live in one. This let me live in a small town, and still be only twenty-five miles from Louisville."

It was all right with Claudia. She welcomed the move.

"I don't have any use for Corbin," she says. "I didn't like it when I was there and I still don't. I had all my trouble with my first marriage there. I can't think of anything good happening there except meeting the Colonel. I didn't regret seeing him sell that place in Corbin. Should have sold it sooner. Two years before, he had standing room only; then they rerouted the road and he almost gave it away."

The Colonel loaded a few pressure cookers, a couple of timers, and packages of his secret herbs and spices into the trunk of his car (legend has it that it was an old Ford; actually, it was his usual white Cadillac), and early one morning, hit the road. He was sixty-five years old. His arthritis was hurting him more and more. But there was too much Harland in Colonel Sanders to be content with Social Security. He told himself that he could, and would, make one more start.

"Hell," he said. "I had to."

8

Selling, as any good salesman knows, is something of an art. It involves considerable acting and, like acting, is an emotional exercise. The salesman who is depressed, discouraged, or sick, the salesman who doesn't really believe in his product, is not likely to make many sales. Like an actor waiting in the wings for his cue, the salesman must psych himself, convince himself of his own ability and the quality of his product, and get himself into the proper, positive mood before he goes out to transmit his emotions and convictions to his audience—or to his prospect.

Colonel Sanders knew this. He had spent nearly half a century in selling, and he knew that, regardless of the product of the moment, what he was really selling was himself. He knew that he had enough self-confidence, a belief in his ability to perform his role. He believed deeply in his product. But there were moments, during those first months on the road, when he had to fight back the gnawing pangs of doubt.

Worst of all was the temptation to quit. And he could have quit if he had wanted to. Despite all of his talk about being "broke at sixty-five," he had quite a cushion to fall back on—a home, a car, some savings, insurance, Social Security, and a trickle of income from the franchises he had given out. These thoughts occurred to him at the end of a long day, when his joints ached and when some restaurant owner was too busy to listen to his proposition.

He was, after all, at an age when most men are beginning to spend their days in the sun, dangling a line off the pier. He had led a hard, strenuous life, and the fights and disappointments and long hours of labor were starting to tell. He had to wear his glasses all the time now, and the arthritis that would plague him the rest of his life was hurting, and he had only aspirin for relief, aspirin and pep talks, as he drove along the dreary Midwestern roads, looking for restaurants where the owners would have enough gumption to see the golden future in Kentucky Fried Chicken.

Put yourself in his place for a moment, driving those rain-wet roads, trying to keep accounts in the car seat, worrying about money. It's hard, toward the end of the day, to convince yourself that you're not old, that you're not getting tired. And it's cold at night when you sleep in the backseat of the car in some deserted parking lot to save the cost of a motel, making yourself think of something else than home and a warm bed. You feel a little sick and your muscles ache when you wake up in the morning, wondering for a moment where you are, with rusty eyes and a dry stubble and the old ache in your hands and your white suit all rumpled.

So you wait for a filling station to open and go into the restroom and shave, and throw cold water on your face and comb your hair. And you stand in front of the mirror and give yourself a silent pep talk, and maybe pray a little, and take a deep breath and get ready to go out there and sell this guy, trying not to notice when he looks at you as if to say: What the hell is this, anyway?

"It was right hard going for a while," the Colonel admitted

later (though it was probably not as touch-and-go as he pretended; the Colonel was always building his own legend). It is quite true that a run of bad luck could have ruined him at any time during that crucial first year, but he was building a substantial operation to make sure he did not fail.

At first, KFC operated from the Sanders home on Louisville Road. Claudia ran the office, but mainly answered the phone and relayed messages. The Colonel rented space in a warehouse in Shelbyville, from which equipment and supplies were shipped to franchisees; there wasn't a lot of business for the first six months or so. The Colonel had a woman in Corbin doing his bookkeeping, but she didn't want to come to Shelbyville, and for a while records and bills were just piling up.

Lee Cummings, the Colonel's nephew, and Harland Adams, his grandson, were both working in the Shelbyville office now, handling the shipments. Lee had a friend named Roy Johnson, and he hired both him and his wife Nell to help out. Nell was the first office manager, or secretary, or bookkeeper—titles were pretty vague in those first months. After a few years, the Colonel hired Maureen McGuire, and she finally brought some order to the place, as well as brass and drive.

One continuing trouble with the Colonel's operation was that he tried to do too much himself, instead of delegating responsibility and authority. He was on the road ninety percent of the time, but he hadn't specified anyone with overall authority over home-office operation. He needed a storage and warehouse building close to the office, but it took him months to get around to building one, and his methods, when he did, were typically atypical.

"He had this big old barnlike garage building back of the house there," recalled Maureen McGuire, "and it was crammed full of all kinds of machinery, lumber, stores, junk. One day he announced he was going to have it torn down, and he and one of the men started clearing the stuff out of it. They carried stuff out of there all day long, and finally the Colonel got hot and tired and mad and said, 'The hell with it, that's enough,' and just pulled out a pack of matches and set the thing on fire.

Burned it to the ground. Almost set the house on fire, too. Had
to call the fire department. (He was a firebug, you know.
Sure he was. Loved to see things burn. Once he was driving
through Florida, and his car was all cluttered up with newspapers and packages, paper bags, forms, all sorts of things. Got
on his nerves, so he just stopped the car, piled all the stuff up
along the side of the road, and set it on fire. Policeman came
along and he had a hard time explaining what he was doing
burning all that stuff along the road.)

"Anyhow, after they cleaned off the remains, they had the
office building built back there behind the house, the one that's
now Claudia Sanders' Dinner House. But we had things running better by that time."

"It was right hard on the Colonel traveling all the time," says
Claudia, "except that he really liked it. He was gone most of
the time, and most of the time I went with him. I was just as
happy to stay home, but that was his field, on the go. He liked
people and he liked promotional work. He was a natural
showman. Any time he could get out front, promote something, get all the attention, that was him. But once he got it
going, someone else had to keep it going on. He wasn't a
natural manager."

His selling was demanding every ounce of effort the Colonel
had.

"We started out in Indiana and Illinois," he said. "Claudia
worked with me for a while, us doing our act, but then she
stayed home, packaging the herbs and spices. It was easier
with her along, but we saved money me going alone.

"At first, a lot of people weren't interested. Didn't think
chicken could be a big item and didn't want to be bothered
with it. Or some thought they knew more'n me about cooking.
How I worked was, I would go in and offer to cook for the
help, and if they liked it, I'd get to talk franchise with the
owner or manager or whoever. One advantage of that was I
got to eat with the help for nothing, don't you see, and it let
me get in the kitchen, where I could show the cook how. Then
he'd see how to fix the best chicken in the world, and save

time, too. And, well, once I got the cook, and got the help to
say how good it was, usually I could talk to the owner. And I
got myself a free meal.

"Of course, I ate an awful lot of chicken in those days. And
liked it. Yessir. I had to to eat that much and still like it. I'm
just glad it wasn't nobody else's."

The Colonel was not only calling on owners and negotiating
agreements; he was taking part in all sorts of promotional
schemes. He would stage half-price sales at new outlets, giving
away a bucket of chicken for every bucket sold. He found that
every middle-sized town would have either a radio or television talk show, with a host usually hard up for color. In most
cases, he had little trouble getting on the air, and once before
the mike or camera went all out to publicize his chicken, sometimes wandering through the audience handing out drumsticks
or eating one himself in front of the cameras while the poor
host sat there trying to smile and wondering what kind of wild
man he had on his hands.

Sales came slowly, but they came. And out in Salt Lake City,
Pete Harman, to whom the Colonel had given the territory of
Utah and Montana, was also issuing franchises under an
agreement in which the Colonel shared in the revenues from
chicken sales, and got the new customer for his herbs, spices,
and equipment. Mildred was working with the Colonel by this
time, while Margaret and her new husband were beginning
their franchising efforts in Florida. By the beginning of 1958,
several dozen restaurants in the Midwest were featuring big
signs advertising COLONEL SANDERS' KENTUCKY FRIED CHICKEN.
The signs of success were popping up like spring grass, and
with them Harland's old confidence was flowing. By the end of
that year, he knew it was just a matter of time. He was going
to make it big.

But the Colonel was sticking to his guns in the matter of
quality.

"I remember this one time," he recalled, "we heard this fellow in Illinois wanted to talk to me, so me and Claudia got in

Harland Sanders (far right) was about thirty years old and working as an insurance salesman when this photograph was taken with his mother, his brother Clarence, and his sister Catherine.

Harland Sanders and an unidentified person in his first kitchen in Sanders Court, Corbin, Kentucky.

Harland Sanders was a Kentucky colonel, but had not begun to make use of the title when he attended this restaurateurs' convention in 1949.

The first known photograph taken of Harland Sanders after he began wearing his "colonel suit" and growing his mustache and goatee in 1951. Always the booster and promoter, he is shown here on a governor's tour as regional director of the state chamber of commerce. PHOTO: Charles Darneal COURTESY: *Courier-Journal* and Louisville *Times*

In 1965 the Colonel poses with Jack Massey (far left) and John Y. Brown, Jr., to whom he has just sold his Kentucky Fried Chicken, Inc. At right is Don Hines, then director of franchising. COURTESY: *Courier-Journal* and Louisville *Times*

The first pressure cooker with which Colonel Sanders began experimenting with fried chicken at his Corbin, Kentucky, restaurant. It is now on display in the Colonel Sanders Museum in Louisville, Kentucky. COURTESY: *Courier-Journal* and Louisville *Times*

Colonel Sanders makes a point to restaurant owner Robert Orton (left), while his nephew, Jim Sanders (center), looks on. "Colonel Jim" was being trained to take the Colonel's place as "the image of Kentucky Fried Chicken." The Colonel sent him to California to have his hair dyed white. COURTESY: Jim Sanders

Kentucky Lieutenant Governor (later Governor) Julian Carroll and Colonel Sanders admire the historical marker dedicated on the Colonel's eighty-second birthday at the Corbin restaurant where he began serving Kentucky Fried Chicken. PHOTO: Lin Caufield

Colonel Sanders marked his eighty-seventh birthday by dedicating Kentucky Fried Chicken's School of Restaurant Management in Louisville and immediately went into the kitchen to show Robert Poindexter of Salem, Indiana, how it's done. PHOTO: Bill Luster COURTESY: *Courier-Journal* and Louisville *Times*

The Colonel gets an affectionate pat from an older, graying John Y. Brown, Jr., now governor of Kentucky, as the Colonel and Claudia attend the governor's Derby Day Breakfast in Lexington. PHOTO: Stewart Bowman COURTESY: *Courier-Journal* and Louisville *Times*

is favorite black cane rests on a chair as Colonel San-
rs reads a large-type edition of *Reader's Digest*. When
was reported that he walked with a cane, he received
ndreds from around the world. PHOTO: Dan Dry
URTESY: *Courier-Journal* and Louisville *Times*

Business is brisk at the opening of this Kentucky Fried Chick-
en store in 1976 in Wandsworth, a suburb of London. COUR-
TESY: *Courier-Journal* and Louisville *Times*

Colonel Sanders holds Lincoln Tyler George Brown, the son of the Kentucky governor and Phyllis George Brown.

Colonel Sanders inspects the grave site which he chose and designed in Louisville's Cave Hill Cemetery. The bust was sculpted by his daughter Margaret. PHOTO: Bud Kamenish COURTESY: *Courier-Journal* and Louisville *Times*

the car and headed out. It was a long way up there and back, maybe seven hundred miles, but the minute we got there and looked at this place, I knew I didn't like the looks of it. So I went around and looked in the kitchen and it was the dirtiest, blackest, greasiest place you ever saw, and I just said to myself, 'I don't want my chicken in any goddam place like this,' so we just turned around and drove home. I wanted outlets, but I didn't want just any place."

What he really wanted were some prestige restaurants; he didn't get many. But he was picking up more and more of the family-type restaurants and, as he said, their money was just as good as the big places with French cooking.

"He'd be gone for weeks at a time," recounts Maureen Mc-Guire, "and then he'd come barging into the office, hollering at everybody, waving his cane around, cursing, hitting on desks, wanting to know where everybody was, what was going on. Most of it was just for show, I think now, but at the time he just scared the girls to death, especially the younger ones who hadn't worked long.

"I'd been working for Long's Silos there in Shelbyville, worked for him seven or eight years, and it was as good a job as there was in Shelbyville, because in Shelbyville you either work for a doctor or you work in the courthouse, and there aren't many other jobs. I had worked my way up to learning accounting and bookkeeping, so my boss, Mr. Long, could get out and sell silos, which is what he wanted to do, when I heard this job with Kentucky Fried Chicken was open, and a friend of mine told me to apply. Well, others told me not to. They said that 'Colonel Sanders is a wild man; nobody can work for him.' But I figured I might as well try.

"Well, the first time I met him, I asked him, I said, 'Colonel, what kind of a typewriter do you have?' And he screamed at me, just bellered, 'Hell, I don't know, but whatever it is, you'll use it. Damn if I'm going to change again. I get one secretary, she wants a manual. I get another, she wants an electric. You'll use whatever goddam thing we have.'

"Well, that about scared me to death, but I stuck to it and told him I had to have an IBM, but the Colonel was buying our office supplies from this old friend of his down in Corbin, and the man couldn't get the stuff as fast as we needed it, but the Colonel was determined to help this guy out. So it took me a while to get my IBM. I used that manual for a long time."

Maureen did have one advantage. There had been four secretaries, usually of brief duration, before her.

"Each woman had set up her own filing system," she said, "usually in a box of some kind. So in order to set up a central filing system, I had to go back right from the beginning and read every piece of correspondence there had been. That gave me a good picture, the best anyone had, I suppose, of the operation right from the beginning.

"The Colonel would call in and, what he couldn't do on the road, he'd tell me to do. The first time he got back, we just picked up a whole file basket full of letters and went upstairs and he started dictating letters. Funny thing; he always told me he couldn't write too well, with him having no education to speak of. Well, that was just ridiculous. He may have been self-educated, but he knew English when he wanted to. He could write a letter like a Philadelphia lawyer."

Mrs. McGuire had touched on one more curious facet of the Sanders personality: his insistence on appearing uneducated, on speaking as though he had no command of English grammar. Perhaps his folksy, ungrammatical speech ("We wasn't goin' do nothing like that . . .") was intended to be colorful, or to underscore the image of the self-made man. But it was largely bogus. When he wanted to—in speaking confidentially, writing a business letter, or making a speech—the Colonel could use the language with great facility.

"My desk was in the front room of the house," Mrs. McGuire continued, "and the next room, that was the Colonel's office, and next to him Margaret Howerton, who was his secretary then, and then a room for a cousin of the Colonel's, and next to that the office of an advertising man. We pretty well took up

the house until they got the offices built out back. I doubt if
Claudia liked it much. She never had much privacy. She never
complained much, though; never paid any attention when he
screamed and hollered around. She'd just say, 'Now, Harland.'

"The Colonel really had some strange quirks about him. He
hated locks, you know. Hated them. He never said why.
Maybe he just hated the ones that got in his way. I remember
one morning I came to work—I usually opened up the office
—and I came in the front way for some reason, where I usually
came in the back. And since I hadn't come in that way, the
back door was still locked when the Colonel came in. He
worked around for a while and then started out the back door
and found it locked. Well, he started cursing and screaming,
'Who the hell locked the goddam door,' and so on. Then he
stomped back into a back room and came back with an ax and
beat the whole lock off the door. Just beat the whole thing,
broke it off. Then walked out without another word. What he
hoped to accomplish with that sort of thing is beyond me."

It was apparent to everyone at headquarters that, while the
church conference in Australia may have helped the Colonel's
soul, it had done little for his temper or language. And while
he controlled his temper while calling on potential franchisees,
he still erupted when food or service displeased him.

In the summer of 1961, he and Claudia went into a roadside
restaurant in Illinois for breakfast. It was an attractive place,
but when the Colonel's scrambled eggs arrived, they were not
to his liking. Scrambled eggs were one thing about which the
Colonel was as persnickety as he was about chicken and
crackling gravy. He insisted on large fresh eggs, whipped in a
blender or with a fork in a bowl, with a half-eggshell of water
added to each egg. These were then to be popped into a
lightly greased skillet where the runny part of the egg was
steadily pushed toward the middle with a spatula until the egg
held its shape. Then it was flipped over and cooked for one
minute, leaving it fluffy and with no liquid egg.

The eggs served him in this particular restaurant were not of this sort. They were caked on top, runny underneath, and lukewarm. The Colonel spoke to the waitress, asking her to "take this slop back to the kitchen and tell the cook to scramble them right." When they were returned, he took one look and, with his trained eye, saw that the cook had simply thrown them back into the pan for a minute of heating, leaving them as unpalatable as ever. The waitress offered to take them back again, but the Colonel's patience had run out. Storming into the kitchen with the plate of offending eggs, he faced the cook and demanded to know if he was "the sonofabitch who sent this goddam excuse for scrambled eggs back." The cook took exception to these remarks and words were exchanged, whereupon the Colonel threw the eggs, plate and all, into the cook's face.

The cook, his artistic temperament aroused, charged the Colonel with a butcher knife. The Colonel grabbed a stool and fought him off, retreating toward the dining room, where the customers were treated to the unusual sight of a white-haired man in a colonel suit holding back a knife-wielding man with a stool. Neutrals, including the manager and Claudia, parted the combatants. Claudia was mortified, and the Colonel agreed, once the heat of battle had cooled, to register his protests in a more conventional fashion.

By the end of 1960, the Colonel began to sense that he was sailing with a wind that could become a hurricane. He had more than two hundred outlets, including some in Canada, where he established a separate corporation to handle Canadian business. His profits, before taxes, amounted to more than $100,000. He had to hire a supervisor for the distribution plant, an accountant, three packaging helpers, and office workers.

He bought a gold-colored Rolls-Royce and had his likeness and the words KENTUCKY FRIED CHICKEN painted on the sides in dazzling blue-and-white. Most Kentuckians, including the people of Shelbyville, were still not aware of the increasing popularity of the Colonel and his chicken, and they joked about "that weird Sanders guy," and "the only Rolls-Royce in the world used as a chicken coop."

"No one knew what kind of business we were running," recalls Maureen McGuire. "We weren't making anything, and they couldn't see that we were selling anything. There was no way for people to know what was going on. I'd go to make deposits in the bank, and the cashier said to me, 'You people have the biggest deposits of anybody doing business with the bank here, unless one of these people sells a big farm.' They were really curious about it."

But things were getting almost out of hand. KFC was getting to be a very big business. It was developing sideline enterprises. Mildred became active in Colonel's Foods, a subsidiary formed to make and distribute such things as sauces, syrups, and candies. Maureen McGuire started Maureen McGuire, Distributors.

"The Colonel didn't have time to mix the seasoning, and he hadn't then made a contract with a company to do it for him, so I set up my company to mix and box and distribute the spices to franchisees on order. I mixed and packaged it in my garage, and I peddled it around, put it in the back of my car, and when I had off days I'd go around and sell it to restaurants. The Colonel told me that when they got Colonel's Foods going, I could have stock in it, too. But then the franchisees began to complain about me selling seasoning to people who didn't have a franchise, and said they'd just give up their franchise if anybody could buy it, so we washed out Maureen McGuire. I got stock in Colonel's Foods, and when that was discontinued, I was given stock in KFC, which pretty well set me up, though I didn't know it then."

Though he was beginning to operate on a big scale, the Colonel still had his heart in the kitchen. He felt that his success stemmed from the fact that he offered an honest product, and he worried that his franchisees would not follow his recipe precisely. He found some selling french fries instead of mashed potatoes. Others were not following his directions for making the gravy—and he was even more sensitive about his gravy than he was about his chicken.

He gave up his old practice of sealing an agreement with a handshake, and had a formal contract drawn up giving him the right to inspect premises and personnel and to withdraw rights of Kentucky Fried Chicken if he found his rules being violated. He found a franchisee using powdered eggs instead of his prescribed "large fresh eggs" for the "warsh" in which the chicken was dunked. He threw a fit.

Twice men called on him offering to buy him out, both associated with drugstore chains. He did not consider the offers seriously. But the size and scope of his operation had made him begin to consider delegating more of the authority. He was now having real trouble franchising, policing his franchisees, running the Shelbyville headquarters and distribution facility, teaching at the regional schools he was setting up, checking on the books, hiring new people, and grappling with taxes and corporate laws. He and Claudia began to wonder if they would ever get to relax, travel, and enjoy what they had built.

By 1963, the Colonel had over three hundred outlets. His revenues passed the half-million mark. He was also becoming something of a celebrity. But while he publicly conducted himself with a dignity and presence as the Colonel that Harland could never have achieved privately, he had to admit it was costing him a high price. He was putting on weight. For the first time, he began to admit he was tired at the end of a long day. And while he would not admit it even to himself, he knew that he was excited when he got an offer to sell out.

One day in Lexington, he ran into John Young Brown, Sr., his old political friend from Corbin days. Brown, by this time, had run unsuccessfully for governor, for the U. S. Senate, and for governor again, had been elected to the state legislature and later defeated as an incumbent, and had finally settled down to a lucrative bluegrass law practice. They reminisced about the days when Harland was pumping gas and cooking country ham, and the Colonel told in some detail of his subsequent success.

"Tell you, John," he said, "I need a lawyer. I don't guess you'd consider coming to work for me, would you?"

"No, Colonel," Brown said. "I'm not your man. I have my son-in-law in the firm with me now, and I wouldn't want to limit myself to being a corporate counsel. Tell you what, though. You know my boy, John Y. Jr.? He's in practice over in Louisville now. Just opened his office. Why don't you go see Johnny?"

The Colonel said he would.

9

At twenty-nine, John Young Brown, Jr., was a tall, handsome, athletic, energetic, bright young attorney with a beautiful wife, three handsome children, and a law practice which few people thought would amount to much. Their skepticism was based on the belief, common among those who knew him, that the law would prove too dull and slow a path to the top for the restless, ambitious Lexingtonian. John Y., they said, was too much the salesman, the promoter, the high roller, to be content with the law. Politics, maybe. He had attracted the attention of Democratic pros throughout the Bluegrass State when he appeared on television in support of his father's senatorial campaign, and some newspapermen said that the most interesting thing about the campaign was John's emergence as a potential candidate.

John Y. did nothing to discourage such speculation, though he did little to encourage it, either. Neither did he try to hide the fact that he had his eye on high peaks.

He had cause for his optimism. As one Kentucky politician put it, "John Y. was born with a silver spoon, or maybe a silver horseshoe, in his mouth." And while it would have been unfair to attribute his success to luck, there is no escaping the fact that luck seemed always to be his patsy. He had never known failure, never tasted personal defeat, and the disappointments along the way had been few.

John Y. liked to remind people that he had worked his way through college and law school, which was true. But he was by no stretch of the imagination a son of toil or privation. Born in 1934, the third of five children and the only son of John Young and Dorothy Inman Brown, young John was brought home from room 328 in Lexington's Good Samaritan Hospital, where his mother gave birth to all of her children, to a comfortable, attractive home on Eldemere Road. When he was six, the family moved to the more prestigious Chinoe Road, where John grew up—popular, talented, and self-confident, and schooled in the virtues of hard work and the Christian church. He was also drilled in the virtue of winning, and learned at an early age how to play poker. Well.

Though he recalls his boyhood fondly, being the only son of two hard-driving, ambitious parents (his mother was a champion bridge player who hated to lose) had its pressures. Some family friends thought the pressures were greater than necessary. "I think John and Dorothy put too much pressure on Johnny," said the wife of his high school coach. "He spent the whole of his young life trying to live up to what they expected of him."

From the time he entered school, it was understood that he was to make good grades, and until he entered high school, where he and girls discovered each other, he was a straight A student, helped along by a photographic memory, a precocious knack for figures, and the ability to charm his teachers. "Johnny was always bright," recalls Mrs. Thelma Beeler, one of his teachers. "Maybe too bright. He knew he could make grades, so he didn't study as hard as he could have. But he was a pleasure to have in your room."

Both parents wanted him to be a competitor. God, his father told him, did not put us here just to exist; every man has his talents, and it is his responsibility to make the most of them. If he doesn't keep trying to excel, he will stagnate. The lesson took root. When he was ten, his father told him he should stop caddying and start playing golf on his own. "Okay," said Johnny, and within two years was winning state tournaments. When he was fourteen, he entered an oratorical contest without telling his parents, but in the press of other activities he forgot to write a speech until the night before the contest. Frantically, he wrote, practiced before the mirror, and the next morning won first prize. His title: "Effort Makes Success."

Occasionally, parental pressure touched raw nerves in young John. One day, when he was twelve, his father had been riding him hard at the dinner table until finally Johnny jumped to his feet, slammed down his napkin, and, with eyes brimming, blurted defiantly, "You wait! Someday people won't call me your son. They'll know you as my father!" The outburst did not displease his parents.

John Y. Sr. was not reluctant to throw his political weight when his son was involved. When Johnny became a student at Lexington's LaFayette High School, the elder Brown was shocked to find that the school had no football team, for the simple reason that the principal did not want one. Shortly afterward, a bill was introduced into the state legislature making school principals elective, a move principals had always loathed. Within a week, it was announced that LaFayette would henceforth have a football team. The elective-principal bill was pigeonholed and forgotten. Young John played football. He was also on the golf and swimming teams, and for a while was the state high school golf champion.

By the time Johnny became a high school senior, he had also picked up his father's skill as a poker player, and at the University of Kentucky, where he enrolled in 1951, he acquired a reputation as a high-stakes gambler, as well as a varsity swimmer and golfer.

Not that Johnny bowed to his parents' every dictate. When he was a junior in high school, his father got him a summer job on a road-building gang. After two days, Johnny came home hot, tired, and dirty, and, despite his father's ridicule, announced that he was quitting. The next day he went out on his own and got a job selling vacuum cleaners door to door, and in a week made more than the road job would have paid him for the summer.

"See?" he said to his father. "No sense knocking yourself out for peanuts."

The following summer his father, determined to give him a taste of hard work, got Johnny and a friend jobs on a construction project in Alaska, gave them money for fares, and put them on a train. But they got off the train, got into a card game, and lost the money before they got there. John matched the conductor double or nothing for the fares, and won. In Alaska, they hitchhiked to the job site, and he got a job running a generator. It almost cost him an eye. A crank kicked on him and put a gash requiring twenty-one stitches over his left eye, administered by the camp doctor without an anesthetic. He returned home full of tall tales.

Enrolling at the University of Kentucky, he became a salesman for the Encyclopædia Britannica, and was given hilly, depressed eastern Kentucky for his territory. His friends hooted at the idea of his selling the scholarly Britannica to "ridge-runners," but in his first week on the job he made $500. By the end of his four years at UK, he was making $16,000 a year; when he finished law school at UK he was making $26,000, and was a district sales manager supervising thirty salesmen. Britannica offered him $75,000 a year to join the national sales force, but he turned it down. "I couldn't see selling books the rest of my life," he said. "It was time to do something else."

As a matter of fact, he had already done something else— several things. During law school, his career had been interrupted for a stint in the Army. He was sent to Fort Knox,

Kentucky, where he found the experience "pretty interesting, believe it or not," and was chosen by his officers as the battalion's outstanding soldier. While in law school, he began to date Eleanor Durall, an undergraduate from Central City, Kentucky.

"Boy, that was some courtship," she remembered. "On our first date, I waited in the car all day while he called on prospects. On our second, he promised to take me to Louisville to dinner and a concert. I got a ham sandwich." They were married on September 17, 1960, and John went into law practice with his father in Lexington, then quit to form his own firm in Louisville "because I didn't want people to think I was riding Daddy's coattails."

He didn't do badly in his first months, winning nine of ten cases, but as he later admitted, he didn't know much law, or care much about it. He jumped back into politics ("Hell," he said, "I never jumped out"). He headed John F. Kennedy's campaign in Kentucky, and later directed the Young Democrats for Edward Breathitt, when Breathitt beat the veteran A. B. "Happy" Chandler and was elected governor.

Each year, on the morning of the day of the Kentucky Derby, the governor of Kentucky gives a Derby Breakfast. Originally a small, formal affair for a few state dignitaries and visiting celebrities who were willing to travel to the governor's mansion in Frankfort for scrambled eggs, country ham, beaten biscuits, strawberry preserves, and, sometimes, mint juleps, the breakfast grew. Through the process of political accretion, it grew to monstrous proportions, and it has become necessary to move the festivities from the mansion to special tents pitched on the lawn. As early as seven o'clock on the fatal day, the first of ten thousand politicians, hangers-on, tourists, gapers, and just plain citizens start lining up to shake the governor's hand, speak to his wife, eat to the tune of various bands, and watch politicians gladhand each other. For the politically inclined, it is an occasion much like the boss's party, which few like but all are afraid to miss. And it was here, on Derby Day, 1963, that John Y. Brown, Jr., met Colonel Harland Sanders.

"We were both busy shaking hands," John recalls, "so I told him, 'Colonel, when the campaign is over'—I was working for Ned Breathitt—'I'll come down to see you.' So I went over to Shelbyville one day, and he wanted to hire me as his lawyer to handle real-estate matters. I didn't know anything about real-estate law, or much about any kind of law for that matter, but we sat around and talked for about three hours. We were in that back office where Claudia's dinner house is now, and he reached into this drawer and pulled out a bunch of checks, royalties people were paying him to serve his chicken. Some were paying $200, $300 a month. Well, I know enough to know that, at five cents a serving, that was a lot of chicken. It was the first time I had realized the size of his business. I asked him what kind of sales force he had and he said, 'Hell, I got no sales force. If people want to sell my chicken, they can come to me now. I don't have to go to them.' I said to myself, 'Brown, you better pull up a chair and sit in.'

"That evening we were sitting around and he started talking about his plans for starting a new chain, a barbecue chain. He was always having new ideas for different products. I didn't know anything about barbecue, but I was interested in the promotional aspects of the business. I wanted to be involved in the franchising. So I told him I'd raise the money and put up the barbecue place and we'd be partners, and he agreed."

The Colonel later said that he lent Brown the money to go into the barbecue house, but Brown says this is not so.

"The Colonel lent so many people money to go into the chicken business, he forgot," he said. "I didn't want to borrow money from him because I didn't want to be obligated to my own partner, and because he had the kind of personality that he would remember it and expect you to be grateful. He was generous, but he was touchy."

John began studying site-location and franchising. He found a vacant store on Louisville's Preston Street, rented it for $175 a month, and began remodeling.

"My buddies laughed at me because the store had housed a furniture store, a plumbing store, and an appliance store, and all of them had gone broke. It was next door to a funeral home and across the street from a cemetery. But the rent was right."

John got a contractor he was defending in a murder case to remodel the place and do the wiring. He got another client to do his brickwork and make his barbecue pit. He and his wife Ellie painted the place, and Ellie made curtains for it.

"Funny how things turn out. I needed financing. Had no idea where to get it. About that time a young man named Jim Cavanaugh moved into offices above mine in the Kentucky Home Life Building—he was married to a girl named Cindy who had been Ellie's roommate in college, so I went up to welcome him, and we got to talking. I told him what I was trying to do—we were both just starting out and hustling—and he said he would introduce me to a fellow from Nashville who might help me. He was the one who introduced me to Jack Massey."

Massey and Brown took to each other instantly. At sixty-two, Massey was, as Brown said, "having some withdrawal symptoms about retiring," and looking for something in which to invest some of the money he had made in the surgical supply business. John needed $16,000; Massey liked his confidence and aggressive manner. But they butted heads over the matter of the interest Brown was to pay on the loan. Massey wanted six and a half. "I didn't know a damn thing about interest," Brown said later, "but I had heard somewhere that you oughtn't pay more than six percent, and was hanging tough. We argued for six hours over that half a percent. I finally got six."

Massey went back to Nashville, and Brown began looking for someone to operate his barbecue store. And somehow, in the strange turning of coincidence, he came up with the name of Ona May Stewart.

"I don't know who told me about Ona May," he said. "I don't think it was the Colonel, although they'd had a lot to do over the years. She was married to Claudia's brother, H. F. Leddington, you know, and then divorced him, managed

Sanders Court for the Colonel, and then had her own place. I remembered her from the time she ran the Colonel's restaurant over in Lexington. She sold it when she got hurt real bad in a car accident in 1961, and when she got well she married Joe Barbati, who was managing the Tradewinds Restaurant in Lexington. Nice fellow. They both knew what they were doing. I was lucky to get them. We became partners.

"Joe was making seventy-five dollars a week at the Trade-winds at the time, and I offered him seventy-five dollars and we'd be fifty-fifty in the store. To tell the truth, I wasn't interested in the store except as a launching pad. My contract with the Colonel gave me the right to franchise that barbecue any-where I wanted to. It also gave me the right to sell Kentucky Fried Chicken, and if you read it one way, the contract gave me the right to franchise Kentucky Fried Chicken worldwide. But that was the way I was aiming; I wanted a good-looking, successful store that I could show people that I was trying to sell franchises to. I was interested in franchising, not selling barbecue."

John and the Barbatis reached their agreement. They decided to name the store the Porky Pig House.

The Colonel took a great interest in the Porky Pig House, which was not an unmixed blessing to John Y.

"I don't know how much the Colonel knew about barbecue," said John, "but, like in everything else, he knew how he wanted things done, and he didn't mean maybe. He came in one day when the bricklayer who was building the barbecue pit was just knocking off for the day, and the Colonel began scowling and nosing around the pit, then he began muttering to himself, and finally he took his cane and just pushed the whole thing over. Wrecked it. I thought I'd die. I was operating on a shoestring, and here he was, breaking up hundreds of dollars' worth of work."

Once in operation, Porky Pig House didn't exactly set the woods on fire. John Y. had been studying franchising costs and procedures, hoping to start a nationwide system of Porky Pigs, but his pilot operation wasn't doing a land-office business, at least not in barbecue. After the first couple of months, the place was breaking even, but little more.

"It took me about sixty days," said Brown, "to realize that I was in the wrong end of the right business. Because in spite of all our emphasis on barbecue, all the advertising, the name, the big sign, the smoke panel, and barbecue pit, I found we were selling twenty percent barbecue and eighty percent chicken. It occurred to me that when I went into the store, I ate chicken myself. And it was damned good chicken. Well, it didn't take any genius to see that chicken was the way to go."

While John was trying to figure out how to shift gears from barbecue to chicken, the Colonel was running himself ragged trying to manage what was becoming a very big business.

"At first, we kept everything in the warehouse," said Maureen McGuire, "and shipped direct to the franchisee, usually by truck—pressure cookers, warming ovens, filters, seasonings, all the supplies like buckets, napkins, spatulas. The Colonel designed and built everything from buckets to baskets to racks, knives, spatulas—everything. And if a man got a franchise, he bought from us, and nobody else.

"The spices, seasoning, came in twenty-six-ounce bags, little plastic bags. That would mix with twenty-five pounds of flour, or about one ounce to a pound. A franchisee would call in or write in and order so much seasoning and so many buckets, and I would write up the order and put it in the basket and Harland—that was Harland Adams, Margaret's son, he was working at headquarters then—he would come by and take it to the warehouse and ship it out.

"But that got to be unhandy, and we got Durkee's Foods to mix the spices, and then when we got bigger we had a contract with Stange, in Chicago, and they not only mixed and bagged it but they'd send it out direct to the franchisee on our order. And then, after a couple of years, we got Stange to put the seasoning right in the flour and ship the flour to the franchisee.

Some franchisees used our flour, some didn't. Ours was a little more expensive, because the Colonel would use only certain kinds of flour. He wanted them to use it, but he didn't insist on it."

The Colonel wasn't on the road selling franchises so much anymore. As he told John Brown, anyone who wanted a franchise could just damn well come to him. At the same time, he was promoting franchises in Canada and England, and was spending almost half of his time in those offices.

This added up to a lot of equipment, very expensive equipment. Financing all of those cookers, ovens, and other equipment sometimes strained the Colonel's treasury, and John Y. mentioned to Jack Massey one day that he might be able to do some business with the Colonel, financing the purchase of equipment for the franchisees. Massey liked the idea. John set up a meeting and the two men drove over to Shelbyville.

It was not a propitious meeting on which to base a business relationship. The Colonel took one look at Massey and became cautious, suspicious, and defensive. He grumbled that he had too much to do, that he couldn't spend much time talking to them.

"You never knew how the Colonel was going to react," said Brown. "I had called him and told him that I was bringing this finance person over to talk with him, and maybe that made him suspicious. Jack, of course, was dressed like a banker—conservative gray suit, reserved manner—and the Colonel was barging around in his white suit and all, hollering and mumbling by turns. Maybe Jack made him uncomfortable.

"Anyhow, in a few minutes, before Jack could even suggest some financing to him, he said we ought to go down the street and get something to eat. So we did, and you could see he was still upset over something, pulling on his mustache and looking around the room, and all of a sudden he slapped his hand on the table and snapped, 'Let me tell you right now there ain't no slick-talking sonofabitch going to come in here and buy my company out from under me. Nosir!'

"The funny thing was that Jack and I had never even mentioned buying him out; I don't know whether it had even occurred to us. Lord, I'd just borrowed money to start Porky Pig House. I was just thinking about paying that back."

Obviously, the Colonel had been thinking about selling out. He had had a couple of offers but hadn't taken them seriously, but now for some reason the idea had either become appealing or frightening. Whatever his motivation, he had planted the idea in the minds of Brown and Massey. At first glance, the idea seemed ridiculous. Massey had no experience whatever in franchising or the food business; Brown had just as little, and had no money. Yet the two men began to talk seriously about the prospect of buying Kentucky Fried Chicken, Inc.

"After that first meeting, the Colonel settled down; I think he liked talking to a moneyman. To tell the truth, I think he was sort of confused by all the money he was handling—taking in and paying out—and here was a man who knew how to do it. We didn't know exactly how to approach him, but I've always believed that if you have something to say, the best thing is just to come out and say it, and so one day I just said, 'Colonel, I think you ought to sell us your company.' He blew up, like I expected, and hollered and cussed around for a while. It was all show; most of the time he cussed and fussed it was all put on. He just did it to get people off-balance, or scare them into doing something he wanted done, or maybe just to give him a little time to think. Anyhow, in a few minutes, he quieted right down and said, 'Well, I don't know. I've been thinking about it, and I don't see any reason I should.' So we began talking."

Where John Y. got his knack, his instinct for diplomacy, has always puzzled those who knew his aggressive, outspoken parents. Perhaps he developed it as a necessary tool of the salesman. At any rate, he began to use it now. And he needed it. He not only had to persuade the Colonel that he should sell out his successful and growing business, but he had to keep peace between the Colonel and Massey, who were on polite but not friendly terms. They would never warm to each other. Massey had little patience with the Colonel's fulminations, his temper tantrums and accusations, and the Colonel, in turn, distrusted the cool, methodical, seemingly unemotional Massey. It was John's job to keep everybody talking, but to him and not to each other.

He began by flattering the Colonel, admiring the huge company he had built from nothing. He moved on to the obvious —that the Colonel needed more expert help to guide the company through the crucial period ahead, people skilled in finance and management. Then, as gingerly as he could manage, he began reminding the Colonel of his own mortality. He was seventy-four years old. His arthritis was worse. His eyesight was failing. No one would ever suggest that he should retire, but if he did not begin taking better care of himself, he could fall any day to a heart attack. Then what would become of his beloved company? Who was able to assume direction of it? Or would it be torn apart by franchisees squabbling over control? More important, who would see to it that the Colonel's high standards of quality, service, and cleanliness were carried on? How could he be sure that his company would not deteriorate into a mess?

On the other hand, why not sell to him and Massey, at a price he, the Colonel, set as fair and proper? That would make sure that the Colonel and his family would be taken care of for the rest of their lives, no matter what happened to Kentucky Fried Chicken. Jack Massey could take over the financial management of the company; Brown would put together a management team to guide and promote its growth. And this would free the Colonel to do what he did best, and what he really wanted to do—promote the company, act as its goodwill ambassador, be its image, and ride herd on franchisees to see that they followed his rules and methods.

"There is no reason on earth," Brown told the Colonel, "why you should be wasting your time bothering with cookers and ovens and that sort of thing; anyone can do that. You are one of the great salesmen of the world, one of the great promoters. You belong in front of the public. I'll put you there, where you belong, and make you a rich man to boot."

The Colonel sneered. He snarled. He stomped and grumbled, fumed and cursed. He ridiculed Brown and Massey. But then he grew thoughtful, said nothing. The shaft of Brown's argument was in his heart.

"I didn't know whether I was doing any good or not," said Brown, "until one day I said, 'Why don't we go down to Nashville and talk to the men at Third National Bank?' That was Jack's bank. And to my surprise, he said that might be a good idea. Well, we had lunch in their big boardroom, very quiet, elegant. The Colonel enjoyed it. But I was nervous as a cat, afraid somebody was going to start pushing the old man, saying something that would offend him. The secret, I knew, was to let the Colonel do his own talking. He had to think it was his own idea. He just wasn't the kind of man to whom you could come out and say, 'I'll give you so many dollars.' But, of course, I didn't have any money. I didn't have any leverage. I couldn't tell these guys with the money what to do. I just had to smile and dance around between them and hope nobody rocked the boat.

"After lunch, we talked around the subject, waiting for him to make an opening. I don't think he had really digested the idea of selling. On one hand, it was his first chance to have some real cash. That certainty of big cash in the pocket appealed to him. And I imagine he was remembering the time he was offered good money for Sanders Court and didn't sell and then saw the value fall to next to nothing. He was thinking about these things. At the time, I don't think he had really considered the possible trauma of selling his baby, his creation.

"Then, all of a sudden, just about the way I figured he would, he said, 'Well, I've been giving this some thought, and I think that two million sounds about right.' He didn't say, 'Two million; take it or leave it.' He didn't say, 'What do you think?' He said, 'I think that's about right.'"

Massey, Brown, and the bankers retired to another room. Some of them thought they should counter-offer. Two million, they agreed, was a good price, maybe a bargain. But it went against their grain to accept any offer out of hand, without seeing if they couldn't do better. Brown, ignoring the fact that he had no strength in the group, warned them flatly not to do it.

"You know it's worth two million. You've got the whole world for expansion; you're buying for potential, not what he has here. You go out there and offer him a million and a half, and he'll tell you to go to hell and walk out. If it's worth a million and a half, it's worth two million."

They went back out and told the Colonel two million sounded all right to them, too. He said that sounded good, but before he gave his word, he wanted to talk to some of his people, especially Pete Harman. On January 6, 1964, Brown, Massey, and the Colonel went out to Salt Lake City to see Pete. Strangely, the Colonel seems to have said nothing about his possible sale either to Claudia or to the people at headquarters until he returned from Salt Lake City.

"We had to sell Pete on the theory that someone had to take the company and manage it, otherwise it would get torn between the family, with bickering among the franchisees, and with no one to assure uniformity, fairness to franchisees. Without leadership, the franchisees would end up by taking over the company and fighting each other. He agreed with that. We asked him how much he wanted to buy in for and he said five percent. The next morning we met at six o'clock at Harman's State Street Cafe, and signed a contract to buy Kentucky Fried Chicken, Inc."

On the way home, the trio went by Cleveland to talk to Kenny King, another of the early franchisees whom the Colonel trusted. King made no objection to the sale, and, like Harman, offering to buy into the new company for $5,000.

"We had a valid contract," said Brown, "but I knew that the value of it rested on the desire of the Colonel to go through with it. He was the symbol of the company, far more, I think, than even he realized. Everything depended on whether or not he wanted to do it. We paid him $50,000 down. I had to come back to Louisville and borrow $10,000 to pay my share.

"So we had a yellow piece of paper. Jack had his attorney come up from Nashville to draw up the formal contract of sale, and he said it would take him sixty to ninety days to have it ready to sign. I almost died again. I knew the Colonel would start talking to people and they would have his mind changed fifty times in ninety days. I said to this lawyer, 'Why can't we just sit down and draw up a contract?' And he said, 'We have to draw up stock powers and releases and penalty clauses and I want to do it right.' It took him six weeks. I was nervous, frustrated. This was the biggest opportunity I had ever had, and I was afraid someone would come in and say, 'Colonel, why in the world are you selling your creation?' I could just see him blowing hot and cold, backing out, saying, 'The hell with it,' just because some lawyer couldn't write a contract."

And people were beginning to close in on the Colonel. As soon as the word got out around headquarters that he was talking to John Y. about selling the company, his friends and associates began to plead with him not to sell. Some of this, of course, was simple self-interest. But others, who had been with the Colonel for a long time, genuinely hated to see him let go of the organization he had built so painfully, just as they did not relish the idea of working for strangers.

"He had talked about selling," said Claudia, "and I said to him, 'If it was me, I wouldn't.' I said, 'You're well enough off, what do you want to get rid of it for?' He never had an answer to that.

"They talked him into going out to Salt Lake City, said they wanted him to talk to Pete Harman, but what they really wanted was to get him away from me and talk to him by himself, and that's what they did. Maybe he got tired, and thought he'd see what somebody else could do with it."

"A lot of people have asked me why he sold it," said Maureen McGuire. "And, of course, I have to guess. But I think one

thing was that he didn't have anyone to inherit the company
that he could trust to run it the way he wanted. Claudia was
smart, and a good businesswoman, but she didn't want to run
it. Margaret couldn't. Margaret and Lee and Harland each
thought they should be running things, but they couldn't get
along together. It was a lot like Mr. Brown said, if the Colonel
died, the company would just go to pieces.

"I felt for him during that time he was trying to decide to
sell or not. He'd come barging into the office, cursing and
bellowing and scaring the new girls to death. I finally went
into his office and told him, 'Colonel, you ought to be ashamed
of yourself, scaring people like that.' And he sort of grinned,
and said, 'Oh, it don't mean anything.' And he looked at me
and said, 'It sure don't mean anything to you. You're from Lee
County; you don't have enough sense to be intimidated.'"

Under the formal agreement signed on February 18, 1964,
the Colonel was to receive $2 million for Kentucky Fried
Chicken, Inc. Of this, $500,000 would be paid by April 16,
1964, and the remainder over a five-year period. In addition,
the Colonel would be made a director of the new company,
and would be employed by the company at a salary of $40,000
a year (later raised to $75,000 and finally $125,000 a year) to
act as public relations man and goodwill ambassador, to appear on television commercials, open outlets, and publicize the
company image. This last provision was a brilliant stroke by
John Y. Brown, Jr. Massey was not eager to have the Colonel
around; the Colonel was no admirer of Massey. The two men
were simply too different to appreciate the talents each
brought to the company. But Brown realized that the Colonel
was "not just the image; he was the company." And the provision of the contract employing the Colonel as public relations
man and goodwill ambassador not only persuaded the Colonel
to sell, but gave Brown the combination of image and product
that paved the way to success.

It is worth noting that the Colonel did not sell everything.
He kept the rights to Canada (he had formed a separate
Canadian company, and later gave all Canadian profits to

charity); Florida, which he had given to Margaret; Utah and Montana, where Pete Harman had franchise rights; and England.

But for John Y. the anxious time was not over. The deal was not final until the Colonel actually accepted payment, and there were times when it appeared the Colonel was about to change his mind. He began to realize that his creation really was about to be taken from his control, and in his rare moments of looking back, he wondered if he was not in a sense selling his life's work and losing, in the process, his reason for being. He watched Brown begin to gather his team of new faces, most of them men who seemed to the Colonel too young to know what they were doing. He objected to almost everything Brown was doing. He stomped out of meetings with veiled threats to call the whole thing off.

"One day, it occurred to me that there had been nothing at all in the papers about the sale," said Brown. "So I called the *Courier-Journal* and told the business editor that there might be a story in it. A reporter came out and wrote a big front-page story about Massey and me buying out the Colonel for millions of dollars. It made a big splash and, a funny thing, once the Colonel saw the story in the paper, he seemed to quit stewing about it and accept things."

In April, on schedule, he took the money, and undertook for the first time to be a member of a team. The transition was not easy. The negotiations had produced a lot of ruffled feelings. And there was pathos in the letter he wrote, on November 15, 1965, thanking Brown and Massey for a gift they had made to his beloved Salvation Army ("They give a break to the down-and-out fella," he said).

"It is my intention," the letter read, "to deliver to you the best and most conscientious service I can render, consistent with my health, as long as I remain on your payroll. I can see no cause for anything ever arising again to cause the heartbreaks we have endured for the past eighteen months. The business is yours to operate as you please, and I will never be critical to anyone other than you two about how you operate it. Anything that I suggest to you would be merely a suggestion, and no hard feelings on my part if they are not taken. I wish you both health and happiness from this day on."

It was a generous, gracious, almost noble statement, coming as it did from a man of the Colonel's fierce individualism and fiery temper. It was also, it must be added, a very emotional statement, more from the heart than the head. His resolution to keep his criticisms private melted within weeks, and the Colonel was once more brandishing his cane and denouncing the new owners who were ruining his company.

John Y. and Massey, meanwhile, had met and decided on the management structure of their new company. Remarkably, they had never discussed, much less reached agreement on, how the stock, offices, and control of the company were to be divided.

"Jack and I had had a handshake in Salt Lake City, and that was all," Brown recalled. "I told him I thought we could work out something fair to both of us for what I had contributed to putting the company together, and that I wanted to help run it.

"I remember walking into the den there in my Louisville home and saying, 'What do you think is fair?' And it always impressed me that he turned it back and said, 'What do you think is fair?' I told him, off the top of my head, I thought a sixty-forty split would be fair, with him getting the sixty, and he said, 'That sounds good,' and we shook hands on it. Took about fifty seconds. That gave me a world of confidence in the way to do business, and we had a great relationship for eight years. The only disagreement we ever had was over where the home offices were to be located. I thought Kentucky Fried Chicken would be in Kentucky. He wanted the offices close to him in Nashville. And it was his money.

"We signed the final contract in Nashville—Jack, the Colonel, and I. The Colonel was going to sign it without reading it—on faith—but Jack said, 'No, I want you to read every paragraph and discuss it and be happy with it.' I knew that was right. We didn't want him saying later that he had been fooled by small print, that there was something he hadn't understood. We finally got it signed, and Jack came over to me and said, 'John, this is going to make you a millionaire.' I couldn't picture that. I had hoped to make, oh, maybe $100,000. I couldn't quite figure a million."

Actually, it would make him many, many millions, and it would make millionaires out of dozens of the men who followed him into the growing company. But, first, he would experience a small bit of irony.

Now that he had control of the entire chicken empire, he had little use for his Porky Pig House on Preston Street. He offered to sell it to Ona May and Joe Barbati, but they had put most of their cash into their original transaction, and he offered to borrow the money and lend it to them for the purchase. He went to a loan officer at Citizens Fidelity Bank in Louisville and asked for a loan of $25,000, offering to put up as collateral his twenty-five percent of the stock of Kentucky Fried Chicken. Within months, the stock would be worth more than a hundred million dollars. The loan officer said he was sorry, but he could not accept such collateral for a loan of $25,000.

John finally got the money elsewhere. The Barbatis bought Porky Pig House and it is still very profitable.

10

News that John Young Brown, Jr., had taken over Kentucky Fried Chicken left many people puzzled, others amused. Few people, even in Kentucky, knew what Kentucky Fried Chicken was. Some had seen that strange old Colonel Sanders driving around in a gold Rolls-Royce with his picture and KENTUCKY FRIED CHICKEN lettered on the side, but few knew what he was up to. As for John Y., he was best known as an amateur golfer and the son of the veteran Lexington politician. What exactly was Kentucky Fried Chicken? And what was he going to do with it?

"I wondered about that a little bit myself that first day," John says now. "Jack and I took over the company on a Monday. Walked into the Shelbyville offices and announced to our seventeen employees that we were the new owners. They didn't seem very impressed; just smiled and went about their business. And we just sat there. That first day we didn't get one phone call. It was eerie, as though we had bought a business that had somehow just disappeared. What we did get was a flood. The creek flooded our warehouse and we lost $25,000 worth of equipment. Massey said, 'Brown, what the hell have you gotten me into?' "

Once the newness wore off, however, John started moving in several directions at once. Much of his first year was spent going from one franchisee to another, trying to persuade them to convert their contracts from the old agreement, which called for them to pay five cents for each chicken served, to a percentage of gross chicken sales. This would protect the company against inflation, but it would cost the franchisees more, and he had to do a lot of talking to sell them. He argued that the franchisees needed uniformity of rules and products to ensure quality upon which a reputation could be built, and that the company needed enough income to allow it to carry out the national advertising and promotion that would benefit everyone. It was to the benefit of all franchisees, he reminded them, to have a company that could provide supervision of outlets, so that everyone would be treated alike and fairly. As evidence of his sales ability, he persuaded over ninety-nine percent of all franchisees to go along with the new regime.

"At the same time, I went out to find some bright, lean, hungry young men. A lot of them were college friends. I told them, 'I'm going to work you to death, but if you stick, we're going to get rich, all of us.' I always believed that a man would produce better if you gave him a stake in the business, so we gave stock to some, helped others buy it. And we started moving. I didn't know how much I didn't know, so we just started selling."

And the chief thing he started selling was the Colonel.

"I figured we had two things to sell," John said (and it is significant that from the beginning he saw his job as one of selling, not managing). "One was a product—Kentucky Fried Chicken. It was not just a good product—it was the *best* product on the market. We knew it was the best. Experience had proved it was the best. It was established. The name was fairly familiar. The people who sold it believed in it and the people who bought it liked it. We just had to get it to more people.

"To do that we had our biggest advantage of all, our image, Colonel Sanders. I knew from the first that he was our ace. He wasn't just a trademark. He wasn't just somebody that an adman had made up, like Aunt Jemima, Colonel Morton, or Betty Crocker. He was a real, live human being, and a colorful, attractive, persuasive one. My job was to get him before the American people and let him sell his own product."

But the Colonel, he decided, was wasting his time introducing Kentucky Fried Chicken, holding two-for-one sales, and appearing on local talk shows. He wanted to get the old man on national TV.

"I got Stan Lewis, a New York PR man, to build the Colonel's image. Stan was perfect—young, creative, and hungry. He did an outstanding job from the first day, but getting the Colonel on network TV proved a job.

"Paul Hornung [former star running back with the championship Green Bay Packers and an old golfing buddy] helped me with that. He knew Toots Shor, the restaurant owner, and he spoke to him, and Toots knew John Charles Dailey, who was in charge of 'What's My Line?' and he spoke to him about having the Colonel on the show. And the thing is, the Colonel was so good on the air that once we got him on 'What's My Line?' the rest was a lot easier. Not easy, but easier.

"I spent almost half my time promoting the Colonel. Over a period of three years, he was on some thirty national TV shows—Johnny Carson, Merv Griffin, 'I've Got a Secret'—all those. We had to come up with a new gimmick each time, but the Colonel was such a great actor that he made things look easy."

On the Carson show, the Colonel appeared carrying a box containing the $2 million he had gotten for his company. He more than held his own in repartee with Carson, who loved him. John Y. got him on "I've Got a Secret" by telling how, when the Colonel had to go to Canada just after he got his two million, he took it and hid it in a can in the garage until he returned. (Actually, he never received $2 million at one time, but it made a good publicity gimmick.) On "The Merv Griffin Show," a man named Burns—from the Broadway play *Hello, Dolly!*—appeared in a Civil War uniform and kept walking up and down the aisles, glancing through the audience. Griffin, who was not in on the gag, asked who he was looking for, and was told "That Colonel who stole my wife, suh!" Suddenly, Burns shouted, "And there he is!" and charged into the audience toward the Colonel, who jumped from his seat and ran down the aisle, followed by ushers pushing barrels filled with Kentucky Fried Chicken, which the Colonel started tossing to the audience, then to Griffin, who stood, aghast, as the Colonel took his show away from him.

"Every time the Colonel would get on one of those shows, I'd get so nervous I'd almost pass out," said Brown, "but it never bothered him at all. He loved it. He was such a great natural actor. We'd be backstage, waiting for him to go on, and I'd keep reminding him to say this and say that, and he'd say, 'John, quit worrying. I know what to do.' And when his time came, he just pranced out there like he'd been facing the footlights all his life. And I guess when you get down to it, that was the secret. He'd been preparing for this all his life, waiting for his chance, knowing what he could do if he had the chance, waiting to act on a stage big enough to fit him."

Claudia began to tire of the crowds, the people who interrupted their meals to shake hands or speak to the Colonel so they could tell the folks back home. But the Colonel loved it. He simply liked to perform. He even appeared in a movie, *The Loudmouth,* starring comedian Jerry Lewis, who became a lifelong friend. They first met after Lewis heard the Colonel's voice on a TV commercial. Though he could not see the set, he liked the sound of the voice, and told an assistant, "Find out who's talking. I want him for the part of the man at the hotel desk."

The Colonel cheerfully accepted the role. It was a small one, in which he played the part of a man trying to check into a hotel, and who was not getting much attention, prompting him to pound the registration desk with his cane and demand service in a loud voice.

He played his first movie role without a hitch. Around KFC headquarters, no one was surprised. After all, they said, it was pure typecasting.

"Every time the Colonel was on one of those shows, sales would jump," recalls John Brown. "It really put us on the map. It not only helped us sell franchises, but it helped the franchisees sell chicken, so that we were making money with them. Our whole concept was almost fantasy, we were so dominanted by one individual. And within five years, we were the fastest-growing company in America."

But the company couldn't count on free advertising forever. Brown needed an advertising budget, and a big one. In 1965, he asked all franchisees to donate twenty-five dollars a month per store toward an advertising campaign. The next year he asked for fifty dollars. This enabled him to create radio and TV commercials, newspaper mats and copy the franchisees could use in local ad campaigns of their own. Most important, it let Brown begin the phenomenally successful "finger lickin' good chicken" television commercials, featuring the Colonel.

Again there was a lot of uneasiness in corporate headquarters and in the New York advertising agency about the ability of the Colonel to perform to the split-second demands of television commercials. The worry was pointless.

"At first, naturally, the television types, the commercial makers, took one look at the Colonel and thought, 'Oh, Lord what have we got now?'" said Stan Lewis. "And then he stood them on their heads. I've had ad agency people tell me he was the best commercial talent they ever worked with. He got the drift of the commercial right away. And he just had a knack for the camera.

"But the boys who were really surprised were the ones who tried to push him around. The Colonel knew a bad script when he read one, and nobody was going to make him do a bad one. He knew exactly what he wanted to do, and he did it. One day this rather effete type said to him, 'Colonel, will you just read your lines like you're supposed to?' and the Colonel looked at him for about five seconds and said, 'Son, if you'll just sit down and shut up, I'll change this thing so it's fit to read. And then,' he said, 'I'll read it.'"

"He was just as much at home in front of a national TV audience," said John Brown, "as he would have been back in Corbin with a two-dollar-dinner customer."

The use of the Colonel as the company's image proved shrewd in several ways. Fronting the massive advertising campaign John launched in the winter of 1965, the Colonel smiled his way into America's awareness. His kindly countenance, beaming benevolence on happily munching kiddies, smiled from every television set. Comedians began making jokes comparing henpecked husbands to a chicken facing Colonel Sanders. The country made "finger lickin' good" its bywords. And when the Colonel told them that his chicken was "finger lickin' good, folks," there was about him an air of genuineness and sincerity that defied doubt or disbelief. America liked what the Colonel cooked, but, first, it liked the Colonel.

Using the Colonel was shrewd, too, in that it kept the Colonel busy, and while this did not guarantee that he was always happy, he was usually too busy to get discontented. Brown took another step to involve the "old man" in the company when he created the Kentucky Fried Chicken University, a training school where franchisees and their cooks were taught the mysteries of cooking the Colonel's way (not including the secret recipe of herbs and spices, which was kept even from officers of the company, lest some schemer use it to take off on a competitive venture of his own). Classes at KFCU were limited to ten students for each five-day instruction period, so that each one of them could receive personal instruction in approved procedures.

The Colonel took great interest in the school, though it replaced the old regional training kitchens, such as the one at Kaelin's, in Louisville, which he had previously used. He was regarded with respect approaching reverence by the students; he was, after all, the man who started it all, discovered the secret. He had made millions, and now it began to look like a lot of others would make millions by following him.

By the end of 1966, the Colonel was beginning to ignore the schedule set out for him by company PR people, and would make surprise visits to franchisees, sampling their fare and raising unshirted hell when it did not please him. There were some people around headquarters that he did not like, some things he did not understand. He was suspicious of men who had never faced a working kitchen or a hungry customer in their lives. He seethed and cursed when, at Massey's urging, company offices were moved in 1965 to Nashville.

"This ain't no goddam Tennessee Fried Chicken!" he stormed. "No matter what any slick, silk-suited sonofabitch says." He operated out of Shelbyville, and went to Nashville only when necessary.

"I could see trouble coming from the day Mr. Brown and Mr. Massey took over," said Maureen McGuire. "They wanted to do things differently, the way a big company had to be operated, and the Colonel wanted to keep on doing things the way they had been done. I said to him, 'Colonel, you really don't expect them to do things the old way, do you? You want them to take advantage of new ways, the way the company is growing.' And he said, 'They don't need to do things any new way. This thing is growing so fast, if they'll leave it alone, it will run over top of them.' The trouble was that it was growing so fast it had to have someone channel it, control its growth.

"The friction between the Colonel and Mr. Massey developed mostly over Nashville, but they just rubbed each other the wrong way. Mr. Massey was a successful man. He had made a lot of money, and he knew how he wanted things done. And when he wanted something done and the Colonel didn't, Mr. Massey just went ahead and did it, and that made the Colonel mad. Mr. Brown was more diplomatic, talked the Colonel into things, tried never to hurt his feelings."

The distrust between the Colonel and Massey often boiled over and hurt those around them. When the offices were moved to Nashville, Mrs. McGuire went along as corporate secretary. The Colonel had requested this, just as he had asked that Mrs. McGuire be given some original stock in return for having pretty well run the company when the Colonel was out of town for so many months. The Colonel was, nevertheless, hurt when she chose to go to Nashville with the new management. But before the move was made, another incident stirred the Colonel to anger that smoldered for years.

The Colonel's office in Shelbyville was in a downstairs room, while John and Massey had rooms upstairs. One day, a long-distance call came for Massey, who invited the Colonel to join the conversation. After a while, the Colonel said goodbye to the caller. But he did not hang up, as Massey supposed, and merely placed his hand over the receiver while still listening on the line. Mrs. McGuire, looking from her desk through the window of the Colonel's office, saw this. She was not only shocked to see the Colonel eavesdropping on Massey's call, but confused about her own obligations and loyalties in the matter.

"I loved the Colonel, and I was loyal to him," she said. "But I was loyal to Mr. Brown and Mr. Massey now, too, and I couldn't just ignore what the Colonel was doing. I went upstairs and told Mr. Massey not to say anything because the Colonel was still on the phone. He said, 'You gotta be kidding; go back and check.' So I did, and the Colonel was still listening in, and I went back and told Mr. Massey, who hung up. But the Colonel had seen me, and he knew what I had done, and he thought it was disloyal of me. Later, he said he had a right to listen in on a call like that. 'If it's something they want me to hear, there's nothing wrong. If they're saying something they don't want me to hear, I need to be listening,' he said. But he was mad at me for a long time over that."

Despite the Colonel's political setbacks and his resolve never again to become involved in a campaign, he was drawn to the glitter and excitement of politics, and in 1964 he accepted the job of fund-raising chairman for the Kentucky Democratic campaign. But he brought howls of anguish from his Democratic friends when, during an interview, he told a reporter that, "I don't think much of parties. I never was a party man.

The sooner the country starts looking at the man instead of the party, the better off we'll be." Aghast, party leaders rushed the Colonel into a hastily called meeting, and rushed out to issue a "clarifying statement" explaining that the Colonel had been misunderstood, that he actually supported all of the Democratic candidates.

It was not the last time he was to prove the despair of the party he was supporting. Two years later, he was again busy raising funds for Democratic state campaigns when his lack of party fervor bubbled to the surface. William O. Cowger, a bright and personable young Republican, was running for mayor of Louisville, and during a press conference mentioned, as evidence of his bipartisan support, that he had just received a contribution of $500 from no less than Colonel Harland Sanders, the Democrats' chief fund raiser.

The Democrats wailed and moaned. Again they rushed into conference with the Colonel, and came out with an explanation that a "secretarial mistake" was responsible for the error. The Colonel wouldn't let that dog lie. Instead, he publicly accused Cowger of "turning traitor to his word," after promising the Colonel that "he wouldn't say a word to anyone." Gleefully, Cowger called a press conference and apologized, rubbing more salt into the Democratic wounds in the process. As a result, John Y.'s Democratic friends asked him to keep the Colonel busy out of the state during campaign years.

But the Colonel was spending little time on politics. His duties as the image of KFC took him all over the country and, increasingly, to Canada and overseas. He was also taking a more active role in such charities as the March of Dimes. He spent a lot of time visiting children's hospitals. Throughout his later years, the memories of his harsh early life prompted the Colonel to give increasing time and money to children. In 1964, he attended the dedication of a chapel and community center built by the Salvation Army in Louisville, largely with his contributions. Two years later, he donated another $60,000 toward a Boy Scouts Service Center in Louisville. In the meantime, he received the Horatio Alger Award, an honor given annually to Americans who rise from humble beginnings to prominence and power through hard work.

But it was not in Harland Sanders' makeup to be content for very long. John Y. was making broad and basic changes in the way things were done at Kentucky Fried Chicken, and some people were bound to hurt, if only because the new procedures were different from the way he, the Colonel, had done things. John Y., for instance, stopped issuing franchises operating out of storefronts; Margaret had had some experience with these, and while the Colonel did not like the idea of having the kitchen out in front where everyone could see it, he was intrigued with the success these storefronts had with carryout orders. In fact, by 1967, almost thirty percent of all KFC chicken was being sold on carryout orders. This prompted John Y. to order a design for a freestanding, distinctive red-and-white-striped building surrounded by its own parking lot and specializing in carryout. Canada was already having considerable success with freestanding stores, although they leaned more to drive-in than to strict carry-home orders.

"I got all the credit for these developments," John said later, "but actually, the Colonel had had the idea for almost every one of them, long before me. That's one thing that people forget about him; a lot never knew it. He was an extremely inventive, innovative, imaginative man. He was always thinking up marketing ideas, publicity gimmicks, sales ideas. You get a man that creative, he's going to be sensitive, emotional."

The Colonel was also very susceptible to suggestion. He still insisted that he put no stock at all in astrology or horoscopes, but he obviously did. In the summer of 1966, while in New York to make television commercials and appear on talk shows, he heard of an astrologer on 57th Street who made up horoscopes and predicted the future, and went to see her during a lag in the shooting.

"I knew about it, but didn't say anything," said John Y. "He was sort of sensitive about it. But one day after we got back home, we were sitting in his Cadillac in front of his house, and he told me he was going to quit the company in August. He was going to quit, go into something else. Well, you can imagine how that hit me. I broke out in a sweat. Naturally, I argued with him. Hell, I was in a panic. I knew that if we lost him we would survive, but I knew that we wouldn't grow the way we would with him.

"We kept talking, and he finally told me that he had had his horoscope made, and that the psychic had told him that he wasn't happy doing what he was doing, and that he should quit in August and go on to a better undertaking, another business where he would be happier and do better. I finally got it out of him where the psychic was, and I got to a phone and called Stan Lewis, and asked him if he knew anything about a horoscope woman on 57th Street, and he said, 'Sure. She's just around the corner.'

"So I told him what had happened, and what he had better do, and he said he'd see to it. A few days later, the Colonel came to me and said he'd changed his plans again. Said, 'You won't believe it, but I just got a letter from that horoscope woman, and she said the stars said I had worked out my differences, and that I should stick with my present job and not quit, so I guess I won't.' I told him I agreed. He seemed perfectly satisfied. Don't know whether he ever went back or not."

Not all of the differences with the Colonel could be solved so easily. John was soon ordering all outlets to be of the familiar freestanding type, with the standard sign and bucket on top, and the huge likeness of the Colonel. When a franchisee opened a store, a company representative was on hand to help and advise. New franchisees could send their cooks to KFCU for $250 per cook. And at least once every three months, a company field man made an unannounced visit to each outlet to see that standards were being maintained.

It was inevitable that some of the new procedures would irritate the Colonel. The new regime leaned heavily on order, precision. He had depended more on energy, instinct, and personal relationships. During his franchising days, the Colonel had made friends with a brilliant engineer from Wisconsin named Carl Mees, who later developed and sold to franchisees an efficient machine for filtering and cleaning cooking oil so that it could be reused, greatly reducing operating costs. Mees and the Colonel spent hours discussing the techniques of cooking, and Mees taught the older man a great deal about the technical aspects of heat application, heat retention and penetration, and the temperatures at which varying changes took place in cooked foods. The Colonel appreciated this, and had assured Mees that he would grant him an exclusive territory.

But he had no contract with Mees, and when John Y. took over he ruled flatly that KFC would issue no more territories. Mees was certainly not hurt in his dealings with the Colonel; he had been a substantial businessman before, and he later made a lot of money selling his machinery for filtering cooking oil.

"But the Colonel felt that John Y. had repudiated promises that he, the Colonel, had made," said Patrick Gorman, who was brought to Kentucky from Milwaukee by John Y. to be vice-president in charge of marketing and advertising. "Actually, John Y. saw that all of the Colonel's franchisees came out all right. But some of his actions, changing policy, made the Colonel feel humiliated in front of his friends, and smaller in his own eyes. And he realized then that he didn't have anything basic to say about how the company was run. And that, as you can imagine, was hard for the man who had built it."

In fairness to Brown, it should be noted that he always treated the Colonel with the greatest tact and patience, partly because he knew he needed the older man, partly because he really liked him. The fact is that the Colonel could never accept the facts of the contract under which he sold his company. That contract turned over to Brown and Massey every aspect of the business, leaving him a role that amounted to no more or less than Brown wanted him to have.

And the Colonel had a restless mind as well as an active ego. He continued, for example, to try to develop a pressure cooking pot that would handle four to eight chickens at a time, rather than the two that the original had held. Carl Mees did develop an advanced cooker, and with the Colonel's help sold quite a few to franchisees. Unfortunately, Brown had at the same time contracted with a Louisville engineer, Win Shelton, to develop a cooker that would handle as many as twenty chickens. Conflict was inevitable.

The trouble was that John Y. was moving so fast in so many directions, trying to ride the whirlwind he had helped to create, that he did not notice that the Colonel was becoming seriously disgruntled.

"When you come to think about it, the Colonel took things pretty well," says John Y. "It wasn't easy for him to sit back and watch other people take over the company he had built, and run it the way they wanted to and not the way he had run it, the way he had made it a success."

"I think H.D. thought that after he sold out, he would keep on running it the way he wanted, and they didn't think that way," said Claudia. "The Colonel was that type of person; he didn't need a boss. I knew it wouldn't work. Not without trouble."

The trouble came to a head at the company's Miami convention of 1967—came to a head and then subsided, all within the space of an hour and a half.

"It was a very important meeting for us," said Brown. "We had had the company for over two years. We were running it. But nearly all of the franchisees and their families were at that meeting, and most of them really didn't know us. They had always known the Colonel, thought of him as the head of the company. This was our chance to show ourselves, explain our policies, make an impression on these people, show that we were in command."

A small meeting on the afternoon of the first day gave a hint that all was not right. The Colonel grumbled, and finally burst out with a complaint that the new management had not set up a pension fund for the employees. His attack took Brown and Massey completely by surprise (they never did discover where the old man had gotten the idea of a pension fund). Did the

Colonel want a pension fund for headquarters employees? For franchisees? For employees of franchisees? "Everybody," he said. "Everybody ought to have a pension." Brown pointed out that franchisees and their employees were not employees of Kentucky Fried Chicken, but that he had already ordered a plan drawn to provide KFC employees with retirement benefits. The Colonel seemed only partly mollified by this explanation. Why hadn't somebody told him about this? Was he or wasn't he part of the management of the company? Jack Massey began to get impatient with this pointless argument, but John stepped in and tried to joke the Colonel out of his bad mood. He thought he had succeeded. He hadn't.

More than one thousand KFC people jammed the convention center dining room that night, waiting to hear the new leaders of the company. John Y. was, he admitted, nervous as a cat. His hands were damp, even as he smiled and took his seat on the speaker's platform. He was tired and tense; he had sat up almost the entire night before, writing his speech. He became apprehensive when the Colonel stalked through the crowd and took his place at the center of the head table: He was dressed, for the first time in John's memory, in a black suit.

The Colonel sat without speaking a word until he was introduced to make what was supposed to have been a brief statement of welcome. John Y. waited for him to finish, eager to begin his carefully prepared report of plans, when suddenly he realized that the Colonel was not making a welcoming address. He was making a tough, tense, thoroughly bitter attack on the new owners of Kentucky Fried Chicken and their methods of operation.

"I couldn't believe it," said Brown. "He said we had forgotten the people that had made the company in the tough early days. Said we were squeezing money out of them, making them pay a percentage of revenue, where he had just taken his nickel a chicken. Said we were ruining the company. That the food wasn't as good as it had been. That we had let quality slip.

"I was sitting on one side of the Colonel, and Jack was on the other. And behind us was a sort of Christmas tree, decorated with checks that all the officers and employees and franchisees had donated to the Colonel's charities—I think the March of Dimes was the main one then. And Jack got red in the face, and said to me with his teeth all clenched, 'I'm taking my check off that tree.' The sweat was running off me, I tell you. I said, 'Please, take it easy. Just wait. Let me handle this.'

"I saw everything going up in smoke. Here, in what was supposed to be our hour of victory, our leader, our symbol, had turned against us. And I knew good and well that if these people believed him, if he left us and turned them against us, our company was shot, just when it looked like it was going to expand over half the world."

Robbed of his speech, threatened with revolt, John Y. got up to reply to the Colonel, and in twenty minutes not only saved his company but removed all doubt that it was, indeed, his.

Brown made no effort to reply to the Colonel's accusations or to argue with him. "What we have just heard," he told the audience, "shows why we have one of the great companies of the world, and why it is going to be even greater. For this man here, who founded it, is an artist, and like all great artists, is a perfectionist. He founded this company on the desire not just for profit but for excellence, and on the belief that if you give your customer the best you can, you will prosper.

"The Colonel," he continued, "wants us to keep up to his standards. What we represent is the Colonel's dream. It really is a dream, and it's up to us to make that dream come true. It may be that in our rapid growth, in our drive to organize this fast-growing company along the lines of order and efficiency that are fair to everyone, we have somehow slipped from following your standards, Colonel. But, Colonel, let me say this: When you sold this company to us, you asked us to be fair and honorable, and we have been. We haven't had a single lawsuit. There is not one single person who can say that we haven't honored every promise, every contract we made. If there is anyone here who has any complaint, who feels he has been treated unfairly, we haven't heard of it, and we want to hear of it."

At this point, the Colonel jumped to his feet, grabbed the microphone, and shouted, "All right! All of you out there who think you haven't been treated the way you ought to be, raise your hands!"

Not a hand went up. There wasn't a sound in the hall. The Colonel hesitated for a minute and sat down.

Brown then went into his report on the increase in sales, the increased price of company stock, the growth of the company, how KFC was now one of the fastest-growing firms in the country, and how they, the franchisees and employees, had made more money from KFC stock than the company had taken from them in royalties. Then he turned to the Colonel.

"Colonel," he said, "you're still our leader. You'll always be our leader. And I give you my word that we're going to make this company all you want it to be and more."

People jumped to their feet, cheering. Tears flowed all over the place.

"Most of the people knew what had happened," said Brown. "They knew it was hard for the Colonel to see control of the company slip from him. They knew how sensitive he was, what a hot temper he had. They knew that he had just shot off his mouth. They were embarrassed for him. But they still loved him.

"The next morning the Colonel came up to me and said, 'Well, John, you did a good job last night.' That was all. He knew he had been wrong. But there was no talk of quitting. Nothing like that. He had on his white suit.

"But that cut the cord. From then on it was ours, and they all knew it was ours. The Colonel was still our emotional leader, our symbol, and we wanted him to be. But we were running it."

11

What would you do if you had a million dollars? Harland
Sanders now had several million. He was a rich man from the
sale of his company. He made a tidy salary, the company now
paying him $75,000 a year to make personal appearances and
commercials, and his television residuals often topped his salary. He owned franchising rights to Canada; he had one hundred and fifty franchised outlets there when he sold KFC, and
the number had grown to more than two hundred. He also
held franchising rights to England.

And he was now the Colonel, not only rich but famous. John
Brown had seen to that. His television appearances, his commercials, his likeness in advertisements and above every Kentucky Fried Chicken store combined to make him one of the
most widely recognized men in the world. Wherever he went,
people pointed, gaped, and waved. Children cluttered around
him. He couldn't step outside his hotel or enter a restaurant
without being surrounded and hounded by autograph seekers.

Every day brought letters begging him to appear on programs, lead parades, donate to or help with charitable drives.

A movie of his life was made, entitled *Portrait of a Legend.* Stories of his struggle and success appeared in hundreds of newspapers and magazines.

The Colonel gloried in it. There was a strong streak of ham in the chicken king. He had always had a love for the flourish, the grand gesture. He liked to make entrances, attract attention. And now he did. Claudia tired of the crowds, the people who intruded upon their privacy each time they sat down to eat in public, and would often say impatiently, "Let's go," when crowds pressed around them wanting to shake the Colonel's hand or get his autograph. But the Colonel seldom refused an autograph or failed to speak graciously.

Indeed, the years between 1965 and 1972 may have been the most satisfying in the Colonel's life. They were also among the most difficult.

He had the fame and wealth that he had worked so hard for, yet he often felt frustrated and at times bitter. The fact is that he had never wanted money as money, and though he now had all the money he could use, he found little pleasure in spending it on the luxuries of life. He and Claudia had the same home—comfortable but not ostentatious—that they had lived in when he began franchising. He drove the same white Cadillac, wore the same white suit. About the only major expense they had that they had not indulged before was for travel, and much of that was done on company business.

Harland Sanders had wanted money because it would let him operate at a level where his talents and abilities could influence more people, and would give him a chance to be the leader he had always believed he was. But though he now had influence, he had little control, and he was a man who liked control.

To the public, he was the Colonel; he *was* Kentucky Fried Chicken. But he knew that he was only the symbol, the image of the company, and that other men were in actual control of it. Other men, many of them men he didn't even know, were running the company he had created and built, and they were taking it onto strange paths.

As he later said in a burst of nostalgia and regret, the company had lost its human touch. He had run the company along very personal lines. He had made friends of his franchisees, and franchisees of his friends. He had lent them money to go into the food business, had given them a product they could sell, and had rejoiced with them in their newfound wealth. They had stayed in his home; he had eaten at their tables. Now, he lamented, they were just accounts.

The Colonel had let his franchisees serve Kentucky Fried Chicken along with other foods. Now the company insisted that they serve Kentucky Fried Chicken products and nothing else. He had charged them a nickel for every chicken they served by his recipe, and let them keep the books, relying on the honor system. Now, he complained, the company made them pay $4,000 just to get a franchise (actually, the franchise fee was $3,000 and an additional $1,000 for each additional franchise). And where he had taken only his nickel, the company now took three percent of sales—for chicken, potatoes, gravy, slaw, and later, baked beans.

The Colonel hated having company headquarters in Nashville. His company had been built on Kentucky Fried Chicken, he declared to anyone who would listen, not something from Tennessee. He refused to move to Tennessee, and made it plain that his personal headquarters were still in Shelbyville, Kentucky.

As a practical matter, John Brown would have preferred to have the home offices in Kentucky, too. He lived in Louisville; his children were in Louisville schools; his friends lived in Kentucky. Commuting was tiring. Furthermore, he believed that it would help the company image to have it located in Kentucky. But Jack Massey had put up the money. He wanted the offices in Nashville, so they remained in Nashville. It was one more factor that fed the Colonel's dislike of Massey who, he said frequently and loudly, didn't know a damned thing about chicken. Trying to get the two men to like or even understand each other was one more task for John Brown, and far from his easiest.

At the root of the Colonel's discontent, however, was his dislike of "the way big corporations act."

"The Colonel's contact was very personal," John Brown explained. "He had the ability to get people to do a job, and his role as head of the company gave him a chance to utilize this talent to motivate and lead. He took a bunch of people, most of whom had never been successful in their lives, and made them make something of themselves. The fact that they had been failures—or at least not successful—was his big reason for liking them. He was the first man to fall for a hard-luck story. The man who had failed and failed, that was his sort of man, probably because he had failed so often and had come back to succeed, and he knew that in a lot of men, buried down there under those failures, are the ingredients of success, if they can just get that one more chance that they need."

And Kentucky Fried Chicken was getting to be very big. Perhaps through the salesman's instinctive sense of timing, Brown had hit the track at just the right moment. The sixties were a time of great ferment. The American home and family were changing, and so were eating habits. There were more one-parent homes, more divorced and single women, more men living alone, and more two-wage-earner homes.

In brief, there were more women working outside the home, and more men coming home to a house without a woman in it. This cut deeply into the old American tradition of three hot meals a day around the family dining room table. After a day on the job, the working woman had neither the time nor the inclination to spend another hour or two preparing a meal every night. Kentucky Fried Chicken gave her a solution, a tasty, hot meal for the whole family at an affordable price. All she had to do was pick it up on her way home.

Furthermore, chicken enjoyed a great psychological advantage over the other forms of fast food which followed it onto the market. For many reasons (ease of preparation, the ability of almost any family to keep a few chickens), chicken had long been the treat meal of the American family. Fried chicken was the traditional Sunday dinner a century before Harland Sanders started frying it with herbs and spices. Herbert Hoover, running for the presidency in 1932, spoke (prematurely, sad to say) of "a chicken in every pot." Country singer Johnny Cash sang of "the Sunday smell of someone frying chicken." And as beef and pork prices climbed in the sixties, both nutritionists and economists recommended chicken as a source of protein.

And suddenly here was the Sunday treat, available for less—per ounce of protein—than the mundane hamburger. It is little wonder that the red-and-white-striped stores mushroomed across the country.

Inevitably, imitators soon pushed into the lush field, but here again Brown's timing proved providential. By the time competition began appearing, Kentucky Fried Chicken had hogged the market. When Americans went to get fried chicken, they looked for the red-and-white store and the smiling likeness of the Colonel. As Brown said, in dismissing his rivals, "They just got in too late." KFC was galloping away with the market, launching the fast-food era, and growing as no other food company ever had, spawning millionaires as it went.

This very success may have been a source of the Colonel's discontent. The resentment, which finally boiled over at the convention in 1967, was undoubtedly fed by the fact that so many people—but not the Colonel—became wealthy overnight when KFC went public in 1966.

"I really didn't want to go public," said Brown. "Not right then. Jack wanted to. I think he liked the excitement of KFC being a public stock, watching it boom. We went up to New York and met with Goodbody and Company and they agreed to take us public, put us on the New York Stock Exchange. I asked them if we couldn't make five times as much if we waited a year, and they agreed that yeah, we probably could, considering the way we were growing. But Jack was pushing for it, so I yielded.

"We had to sell half our own stock in order to have enough to market. The Colonel didn't say much. Said it was our own business. Told some others the stock would probably be worth as much as toilet paper.

"The Colonel had always been very funny about stock. We had tried to get him to take ten thousand shares, and offered to guarantee it against loss. He wouldn't do it. When he sold out to us, we gave him stock as collateral to secure the note we gave him—we paid him two million, but only gave him a half-million then and a note for a million and a half, with the stock as collateral. Well, when we went public, we needed that stock, and we asked him for it. Somehow he got the idea that we were trying to do him out of his stock, even when he was saying it would be as worthless as toilet paper. So he said we could have his stock and sell it, but we'd have to give him sole rights to Canada, which we did. There wasn't any trouble about it."

There wasn't any trouble except in the Colonel's mind. When the stock opened at fifteen and went promptly to one hundred, he saw that he had missed a golden opportunity by not accepting Brown's offer of the ten thousand shares of stock. He regretted it, just as he had regretted selling the company to Brown and Massey. But Harland Sanders had a hard time accepting blame. He had to find someone else on whom to put the blame, and in this case, as in the case of the sale, Brown and Massey were handy.

Not that there were not moments of glory for the Colonel when the company went public. On the day Kentucky Fried Chicken stock was offered, the Colonel, along with Brown, Massey, and officials of Goodbody, walked onto the floor of the New York Stock Exchange, and for the first time in history, trading stopped while everyone on the floor stood and applauded the man in the white colonel suit. Accustomed as he had become to attention and adulation, it must have been a heady moment for the former farmhand from Henryville.

With or without the Colonel's approval, the company went roaring along. Within two years of Brown's takeover, KFC reported a 1966 gross income of $15 million, up from $8.5 million in 1965, and net income of $3.5 million, up from $1.5 million. Per share earnings hit $1.80, up from $.79 in 1965.

The company was growing in many ways. In 1967, Brown bought out Hart's Take-Home, of Houston, Texas, with twenty-five stores, and Ramsey's Take-Home, Inc., of Oklahoma City, Oklahoma, with ten more. KFC was already second only to Howard Johnson among food merchandisers, and it was closing fast.

The franchisees, whatever the Colonel thought, were quite happy. They were making money. As Don Greer, a KFC vice-president who had once been a franchisee, told William Whitworth of *The New Yorker:* "I know for a fact—without any doubt—that if I opened a store in a good location . . . and ran it the way the company teaches you to, I would make money on it. Not just money, but a lot of money. There simply isn't any question. That gives you an awful good feeling, knowing you're invincible."

Brown boasted that no franchisee had ever gone broke, and made every effort to keep that record intact. When a Dallas operator with several franchises began slipping, Brown sent George Baker down to straighten things out. Baker was "a Brown man all the way, a mover, willing to take a chance." A college friend, and one of Brown's encyclopedia salesmen, Baker was also a favorite of Brown for cutthroat gin games. Typically, Brown offered Baker a small salary, but promised him a healthy cut of any increase in income that he could produce. Four months later, he sent Brown a bill for $100,000. Brown paid it happily, called him home, and made him divisional manager of operations. Two years later, Baker was elevated to president of KFC Operations Company and made vice-president of the parent company.

The episode was typical of Brown's method of operation: Get a man who isn't afraid to work and take a chance, give him a stake in the job and drive him hard; if he produces, pay and promote him. It was, curiously, very reminiscent of the methods employed by Colonel Harland Sanders.

In the summer of 1967, Brown did something that made people around headquarters shake their heads. Some say it was just a bit of image-building on his part; others said it was the first and only sign that Brown recognized the company was getting too big for his control. For whatever reason, John went to Harvard Business School and talked with the faculty about the possibility of a course that would give him the knowledge of corporate operation that he felt he needed.

"I was right uneasy about going up there," he admitted. "I had always stood a little in awe of Ivy Leaguers, especially from Harvard. I thought they were so much smarter, had so much preparation, education. The Colonel never did trust New Yorkers or people from the East; most of our stores were in the South and West. So I went up to Cambridge and had lunch with this whole tableful of Harvard business professors, and they began asking me about this little company of mine. I explained that we had bought it for two million and that it was now worth a hundred million, that it had been making three hundred thousand before taxes and was now making ten million. I told them about our stock price increases, outlets, personnel, policies, and so on. And finally this professor looked at me sorta funny, and said, 'Mr. Brown, I don't think there's anything we can teach you about running your company. We suggest that you go on back and keep doing what you're doing.' That gave me a lot of confidence. If the Harvard business people thought I was doing all right, I wasn't going to worry too much."

By 1968, there could be little doubt that his methods were paying off. The stock had split, two for one. An offering of 600,000 shares had sold out at $63. The franchised stores were doing so well that Brown decided that the company should own some of them. He began buying back franchises, and by 1968 KFC owned 136 of them. It would eventually own and operate more than 600. It also listed 1,658 franchised stores plus its foreign operations. Gross sales for 1967 had hit $292 million, and Brown predicted an income of a billion within the decade. In such an atmosphere, there were few people in the company who shared the Colonel's misgivings about the dangers of big corporations.

But if the Colonel had other misgivings, one Brown move in 1968 made him happy: John announced plans to move KFC headquarters back to Kentucky the following year, when Jack Massey was due to retire at age sixty-five.

KFC not only had imitators; it began to have lawsuits with some who became too imitative. A Detroit firm was selling fried chicken under the banner of Kentucky Colonel, Inc. Brown stopped them, to Colonel Sanders' immense relief. The discovery that someone else was using the Kentucky Colonel name had infuriated him. Brown also instituted suit against Kountry Fried Chicken, not because of its name but because it used the slogan "lip-smackin' good," which to Brown sounded a bit too close for comfort to the familiar "finger lickin' good."

A more serious threat surfaced when a Texas chain out of San Antonio, Church Chicken, began showing serious sales strength with franchised stores offering Crispy Chicken. Crispy Chicken was different from KFC in significant ways. It was not cooked under pressure, which produced a tender meat but a relatively soft outside which retained a measure of the cooking oil. The originator marinated his chicken for twenty-four hours before cooking it in the traditional manner. This not only made it tender, but the moisture conducted the heat to the bone, keeping the chicken warm longer without drying out. It had a crisp, relatively dry surface. And people liked it.

Church could, and often did, open its outlets near Kentucky Fried Chicken stores, and franchisees began complaining to KFC headquarters that the newcomers were taking a lot of business. KFC headquarters moved to counter the threat. Pat Gorman was directed to see what made Cripsy tick and to find out how well it was ticking. He conducted a fast but broad and expensive survey of cities where both were being sold, and found that in those cities about thirty percent of those polled actually preferred the crispier chicken, while another thirty percent were indifferent.

Brown decided that if people liked a crisp chicken, KFC

would come out with a crisp chicken. It was that simple. Doing it proved to be not so simple. Adding another line might dilute the traditional image, or imply that the Colonel's recipe was not the answer to all chicken needs. After tossing ideas around, he concluded that it was time to bring out "Colonel Sanders' New Recipe," which would be, in effect, crisp chicken.

The Colonel objected violently. He refused to have his name put on anything other than his time-honored recipe. His "finger lickin' good chicken," he reminded Brown, had been good enough to spark a business doing more than a quarter-billion dollars a year in sales. It was still growing in popularity, at home and abroad. He felt, furthermore, that to deviate from the traditional recipe would be slightly dishonest. He had not developed crisp chicken, or a way to cook it. And he would not lend his name to something that wasn't his, in spite of his agreement, under the contract selling the company to Brown and Massey, to let his name be used on products issued by the company.

The Colonel's attitude posed a major problem. Brown had to keep the Colonel happy at almost any price. He was the company's image. Should he bolt and denounce the company, the result could only be bad, especially if he denounced the new chicken they proposed to bring out. Brown needed to get the crisp chicken on the market quickly in order to meet the competition. But to make it sell, he needed the Colonel's commercials. He needed the Colonel up there on the TV screen saying, "This is my new recipe, folks." Brown knew he couldn't force him, and he knew it wasn't going to be easy to persuade him. In the end, he tricked him.

During the filming of a series of commercials in California, Pat Gorman and his assistant, Bud Allen, offered the Colonel some crisp chicken, without telling him that it was the "new recipe." The Colonel ate it and, thinking it was his own, pronounced it fine. When told he had just eaten some of the "new recipe" chicken (which, he was assured, was prepared with his own secret recipe of herbs and spices), he exploded. He was surrounded, he stormed, by liars, cheats, shysters, and other types of goddam sonsofbitches.

Gorman let him work out his rage (chiefly on Allen) and then persuaded him to sit down and look at the figures. They were disturbing, and the Colonel was enough of an old competitor to know a threat when he saw one. He didn't want to do anything to hurt the company, and grudgingly he gave ground, finally agreeing to do three "new recipe" commercials. He later did three more, but then rebelled. He never really accepted the crisp product. Fortunately, the public did. Today, crisp chicken accounts for one fourth to one third of chicken sales.

Not all ventures were successful. In late 1967, John Brown got the idea for the Colonel Sanders Inns. He had built one in Louisville, near the site of the new headquarters building, and it seemed successful. Why not start a chain?

"Sooner or later, we were going to run out of places to build chicken stores," Brown explained. "So I was looking for other areas in which to expand. I went out to Las Vegas and hired the two top people of the Ramada Inn chain to run the new company."

There were some wild stories about how John hired the two men. One story said that, after persuading them to join him and not wanting to give them a chance to change their minds, he wrote out a contract on a table napkin, signed it, and had them sign. But when he got back home, the Colonel refused to let his name be used on the motels, and John was stuck with a napkin which he had to buy back for a million dollars cash. The truth was actually quite different.

"It was right in one way, though," John Brown admits with a laugh. "The Colonel tried to stop me. He was always insisting that we didn't have the right to use his name in connection with anything but chicken. Well, you can look at the contract and see that he was off base a mile. We had the right to use his name and image on anything we produced, whether it was a candy or a motel. Hell, he did it himself, in violation of the contract. People would come up to him with the idea of using his name on a country ham or a candy or a barbecue sauce, and he would go along and the first thing we'd know, there'd be a new product on the market with our trademark on it. We were always beating out those fires.

"But there was no napkin. I don't know where that story got started. We had a three-year contract with the two men, and we paid them something in addition to the contract. After all, they had left their program, interrupted their careers. We owed them compensation. But the real reason we stopped building the inns, and got rid of the ones we had, was that the investment was too big for return, and about the time we were ready to expand, the money dried up. It wasn't the Colonel, although I didn't want to do anything that he really opposed. But that trouble we had with him over the contract was typical of the trouble we began having from then on. He just couldn't accept the fact that he had sold his company, and with it his name, face—everything."

Brown came another cropper in 1968, when he met Haddon Salt, a debonair native of England who was franchising H. Salt's English Fish and Chips, and had almost one hundred outlets, most of them on the West Coast. Brown and Salt hit it off from the start, and within three months Brown had paid Salt $12 million for his company.

Brown plunged into a nationwide franchising effort, and for more than a year things seemed to be going well. Salt headed local promotional drives, using a double-decker English bus and dressing in the bowler and cane of the supposedly typical stores, and was adding roast beef sandwiches to the menu in some of the fried chicken stores. That effort, too, started well, but faltered.

"John was trying to clone Kentucky Fried," said Pat Gorman. "He had done so well with chicken, he thought he could use the same techniques, the same procedures, and duplicate the experience with roast beef or fish or whatever. The trouble was that he didn't have a Colonel for fish or roast beef. And he wasn't the first one in the field. His product wasn't any better than anyone else's, maybe not as good."

Salt's Fish and Chips ran into several difficulties. People were not familiar with chips and didn't recognize them as plain old french fries. Fish and Chips ran headlong into the Long John Silver's Seafood Shops, which offered a more varied menu and both eat-in and carryout facilities, whereas Fish and Chips was, like KFC, almost entirely carryout. The trouble with carryout fish, Brown discovered, was that fish, unlike chicken, didn't travel well. In chicken, the heated bone kept the meat warm for hours; there was no heat-retaining bone in the fish. By the time people got it home, it tended to be cold and greasy. Cold chicken, on the other hand, was often considered as good as or better than hot.

"One thing we forget," Gorman pointed out, "is the incredible speed with which John and his men could get programs mounted. He built these fish places almost overnight, designed them, advertised them, and began spreading them across the country through that high-powered sales organization of his. They worked day and night, and John used to say, 'Use your judgment. Use your intuition. If we stop to do too much research, it will never get done. Somebody will beat us to it.' He knew he would make mistakes, but he preferred to make mistakes of commission rather than of omission, and the results usually proved him right."

In the case of fish and chips, and of roast beef, he missed. He admitted it, took his losses, and forged ahead. The Colonel was not among those who mourned. Indeed, he had loudly predicted disaster for both ventures, and now he reminded everyone that he had told them so. He had not liked having roast beef in his chicken stores. He had not liked the whole idea of fish and chips. He had never felt at home with the suave, articulate Haddon Salt, though Brown insists that there was no animosity between them. Certainly, the Colonel was not pleased when people around headquarters began referring to Salt as the "Colonel Sanders of fish and chips."

But if some sidelines faltered, the main business was booming. By 1969, the average store had annual gross sales of $240,000, with a profit to the operator of more than $40,000. Many grossed a half-million, with profits of $100,000. It is easy to see how a man with several outlets could become a millionaire in a few years. Many did. So did employees who bought stock in the company when it was getting underway. In 1968, Brown estimated that there were at least 21 millionaires reporting for work every morning at headquarters, among a staff of 280. Maureen McGuire, who had invested $5,000 in the original stock, was now worth $3 million. Pete Harman, the Colonel's old friend and first franchisee, had holdings worth an estimated $30 million.

The Colonel, who had made it all possible, snorted when he heard of all the millionaires spawned in his wake. He had, he said, more than he needed, and there is little doubt that he had more than he knew how to spend. He was spending considerable time in Canada, where he had set up a separate company and a foundation to distribute to charity excess profits from Canadian stores. He and Claudia were traveling more now, and as they traveled they tended to eat, with the result that the Colonel was constantly overweight. He promised to do something about it, but didn't.

During 1968, to the Colonel's delight, John moved KFC headquarters back to Kentucky, occupying a group of one-story brick buildings on Atkinson Square, just off Louisville's Watterson Expressway, while the towering, white-brick, many-pillared, Southern mansion-style KFC headquarters was being built. It was a move Massey opposed as long as he could, but when he reached sixty-five he was obliged to step down and retire. He sold most of his stock, making a huge profit from the relatively small investment he had made less than five years before, and on February 28, 1969, KFC completed the move to Louisville.

"Well, John," Massey said, "I guess you're taking it back home." It was the end, and what some people said was an unfortunate end, to a partnership that had made both men tremendously wealthy and successful.

John Y. Brown became chief executive officer as well as president of KFC. He was now truly in control. Colonel Harland Sanders was elected to the board of directors. He was not especially impressed.

12

For a while, during the summer of 1969, the world was treated
to the unusual sight of two Colonel Sanderses. The public relations people at Kentucky Fried Chicken had been pondering
the fact that the Colonel was pushing eighty, and concluded
that it might be a good idea to have someone to share the
public appearance load, and even perhaps to carry on the
Colonel image in the event the real Colonel should die suddenly.

They thought that in Jim Sanders, son of the Colonel's
brother Clarence, they might have an answer to their search.
Jim was about the Colonel's size. With his white hair and
goatee, and wearing the white suit and string tie, he presented
a fairly reasonable facsimile. If they could get him a colonel's
commission from the governor, they could honestly say that he
was Colonel Sanders. Maybe not *the* Colonel Sanders, but
Colonel Sanders, nonetheless.

"I had wanted to get Jim into the PR operation for some

time," said John Brown. "He looked just like the Colonel: round jaws, portly, white hair, and goatee. And Jim's no dummy. He wasn't as smart as the Colonel, that is, he didn't have the experience, but he had charm, he was presentable.

"I could picture the Colonel giving his nephew on-the-job training. Here's a guy seventy-nine years old, and nobody knowing how long he could last, and I thought maybe the new man can give us a new vehicle. I could imagine two men instead of one walking through an airport. Get on TV and get that much more free press."

The idea did have possibilities. Movie actors have had doubles since movies began. And the strange fact is that a lot of people, though they had seen him munching chicken and licking his fingers on television commercials, did not really believe there was a real, in-the-flesh Colonel Sanders. Even in his last years, the Colonel was often jolted to hear someone say, "Gee, you're real! I mean, there really is a Colonel!" Jim might look younger, but he would, inevitably, age. In the meantime, he would suffice for parades and the like, and get valuable experience in the process.

Jim, who at the time was managing the Colonel's Shelbyville restaurant, thought the idea a little farfetched, but was willing to give it a whirl. He got the suit, trimmed his hair, and made a few public appearances. It looked as though it could be an idea whose time had come. Newsmen covering his public appearances were amused, but commented on the likeness. The Colonel's daughter, Margaret, was indignant.

"I was outraged," she said later. "My father was the Colonel, and he was the only one. Jim was no more the Colonel than he was my father. He didn't have the personality for it. My father was a very definite personality. The whole thing was ridiculous."

There were others, including a lot of people around headquarters, who didn't think the Colonel could be cloned and said so. In the end, they carried the day.

"I let our marketing people, some old maids, talk me out of it," John Brown admitted later. "I think I made a mistake. I think the thing could have panned out. The Colonel didn't object. He wasn't offended at all. He worked well with Jim. I think he liked the idea. It would have given him more time to himself."

It made no difference to the Colonel. He was too busy being himself to worry about a stand-in. When he was not representing Kentucky Fried Chicken, taking care of his own franchises, or overseeing his restaurant, he devoted himself to the charities that would involve more and more of his time, especially charities devoted to children. As long as he lived, Colonel Sanders never tired of children.

He would tour the wards at Louisville's Kosair Children's Hospital and emerge wet-eyed, cursing under his breath at his show of emotion. He would bend or squat down to sign autographs or pat small children, though his arthritis was killing him. He would not leave a crowd of children, no matter how busy he might be, how much behind schedule, or how impatient Claudia might be getting. People at KFC would shake their heads as they told of how he would bellow and curse at someone in his office, stomp out into the lobby, and melt instantly into grandfatherly smiles when a child approached, eyes wide at seeing "the real Colonel."

He kept to a schedule that was, for a man approaching eighty, remarkable. He still made more than a hundred appearances a year for company functions. He and Claudia traveled across the country and, frequently now, overseas. He became a fixture in Louisville's Derby Week Festival, riding in the Pegasus Parade that precedes the Derby, attending the annual dinner of the Loyal Order of Kentucky Colonels, drawing a crowd when he showed up at Churchill Downs. He was beginning to dabble in business ventures of his own. He even attended meetings of the KFC directors, though he admitted that he was usually bored.

There was still some Harland left in Colonel Sanders. For all his success, he was still a basically simple man of simple tastes. Arriving early one morning for an interview at the Colonel's rambling white home in Shelbyville, the author of this book was surprised to find the Colonel knocking the snow from a shovel with which he had just cleared his driveway. "Just got back from Australia last night," he explained, "and couldn't find nobody to do it, and I got to drive over to Louisville to a chamber of commerce lunch today." He straightened up stiffly. "Gave me an appetite," he said happily. "You hungry?"

He led the way to the restaurant behind the house, bustling about the kitchen, instructing the cook, who regarded him patiently and fondly, throwing a chicken wing to a huge Irish setter that pranced about expectantly. Ladling out a huge slab of country ham, dripping with redeye gravy, he explained that "I never eat hog meat any more.

"They're filthy, you know," he said, as his visitor ate heartily. "Scavengers, don't you see? Once saw a bunch of hogs eat a whole load of rotten eggs, rotten as anything. Goes to flesh fast in hogs. Put hog meat off my diet."

But for all his simple tastes, his earthy talk, his preference for direct man-to-man relationships, Colonel Sanders was no longer Harland Sanders. Slowly, almost imperceptibly to those close to him, but unmistakably and indelibly, he had changed. He was at home now among the powerful and famous, able to take success and public adulation in stride. A lot of the bluster was gone, and there was increasing evidence that when the Colonel exploded, it was carefully orchestrated and designed to accomplish a definite end.

"The Colonel was just crafty," said John Y. "He was as egotistical as he needed to be to get a desired result. When he walked into a store and raised hell, he shook people up, but they did a better job. That was part of his technique, part of his selling approach, and he was always the salesman. He'd embarrass a person and then apologize and make him feel good. Oh, he would fuss all the time about things, but he was always a good sport; he'd always end up doing what he should. He cussed and fussed, but that was part of his personality, and I accepted it. The man in the white suit was our image, and he had a right to be different."

The Colonel developed a habit of walking out of board

meetings that didn't interest him, and of skipping them altogether if he felt like it. Some of the meetings were not as dull as he seemed to think. In the fall of 1969, John Brown went to Japan to see if he could spot a market in the small, people-packed island nation. He found Japan "strange but fascinating," and he sensed that there was a market there for Kentucky Fried Chicken. "We've got to adapt to their different ways of doing business," he reported, "but I think it will be worth it."

Japanese custom, as well as the cost of real estate, he found, made it impractical to build the freestanding store, surrounded by its own parking lot. Stores would have to be located on the upper floors of department store or office buildings. "But that's no problem," he explained. "They've got crowds on the sixth floors of some of those buildings thicker than you'll find here in the shopping malls. We'll just go where the crowds are. And we won't have to provide them with parking, either."

On October 9, 1969, Brown announced a fifteen-year joint venture between Kentucky Fried Chicken and Mitsuoishi Shoji Kaisha, Ltd. Mitsuoishi was a substantial partner, a maker of aircraft and a builder of ships, employing two hundred thousand people. It was also, incidentally, the largest producer of poultry in Japan. The first store was an immediate success. Since then Japanese stores have become second-highest in per-store net income.

Brown also announced acquisition of rights to franchises in England, where fourteen stores were already operating, predicting that the company would open a hundred more in the next four years. He also discovered that the citizens and tourists of the Caribbean were being denied the blessings of Kentucky Fried Chicken on the beach, and revealed plans for moving into Aruba, Curaçao, and the Bahamas.

All was still movement, growth, acquisition, and climbing profits. In 1969, Kentucky Fried Chicken passed Howard Johnson to lead all domestic food dispensers, ranking only behind the Army, Navy, and the U. S. Department of Agriculture's

School Lunch Program in volume. In an interview late in November, Brown announced that KFC was studying development of packaged foods, including frozen and other convenience foods that could be packaged bearing the Colonel's label.

Yet the same interview yielded the first hint that Brown might be tiring of the job. Earlier he, along with four other young Louisville businessmen, had bought control of the Kentucky Colonels basketball team of the American Basketball Association, and seemed to be spending a lot of time and attention on it. There had been rumors in the business community that for the first time there was dissension at KFC, and that Brown was dissatisfied with the way things were going. On the surface, all looked as rosy as ever. The company's annual report showed earnings of $12,083,245 on sales of $163 million. But Brown hinted that he might soon be considering other things.

"I want to finish this job before looking too much into the future," he said, adding that, "I'd like to get out of the day-to-day operation and more into planning and acquisition. And," he added, "I guess at some point I'll probably get more active in public life."

All seemed placid, however, until April 2, 1970, which some people at KFC later referred to as "the day of blood." That day, no fewer than four vice-presidents resigned, and the manner of their leaving left no doubt that Brown fired them. The fact was that KFC had long since become too big for one man to run. And John Brown, when he was not speaking to Harvard Clubs or urging Senate committees to institute tighter controls on franchise owners, was to a considerable degree in charge of everything, making policy and decisions on everything from promotion and advertising to prices and new lines. He had felt for some time that his "lean, hungry" young men were no longer lean and hungry, and were not carrying as much of the load, breaking as much new trail, as they should. He had concluded that his young millionaires "were more con-

cerned with their real estate, horses, and investments" than
with the fortunes of KFC. He called a few of them in and fired
them.

"And he did the right thing," said George Baker, who was
one of the departing vice-presidents (he left to found a successful franchising operation of his own). "He needed new
blood. No one could have done what John Y. had done, and
the reason, I think, is that he was completely honest, in products and in personal dealings. You will never hear any of us say
anything against John Brown." (That was not entirely true. At
least one of the departing officials was openly critical, but all
admitted that it had been time for a shake-up.)

As the shake-up indicated, the company, like the times, was
changing, and its needs were changing, too. There was a need
for tighter lines of control, for broader participation in decision
making. But Brown had been deciding, doing, moving on his
own for so long that now he found it hard to give up his direct
and personal involvement in all phases of company operation,
just as the Colonel had found it hard, when he sold the company to Brown and Massey, to accept a changed but essential
role.

A group of new executives joined the firm. But on April 14,
Kentucky Fried Chicken stock dropped to twenty-three dollars
a share. A year earlier, it had sold for fifty-five dollars.

The drop caused worried looks around KFC offices, and
rumors of deep troubles at KFC whipped through business
circles. Brown shrugged it off. The stock situation, he insisted,
reflected the nature of the company's growth rather than any
basic weakness. Both sales and income, he pointed out, were
still growing. But it was unreasonable to expect the company
to continue the growth rates it experienced in the early years
when it was doubling its holdings and earnings with each annual report. That growth rate, he explained, could not be sus-
tained. It had been relatively easy to double the number of
outlets from five hundred to one thousand when the company
was young and small. But by July 1970, KFC had grown into a

network of over three thousand stores. The days of wild expansion were over. The price of KFC stock had been inflated by buyers aiming at quick profits from soaring prices, such as those of 1965 and 1966. The new prices, while disappointing to some stockholders, were more in line with reality.

The in-house uneasiness, as well as public speculation of unrest at KFC, was heightened in August when the Colonel announced that he was retiring from the board of directors. No specific incident triggered the resignation. He had wanted to get off the board for some time. He didn't like meetings. He felt uncomfortable, unable to contribute.

"Now, don't get this wrong," he cautioned reporters. "There is no rift. I just recognized my own incompetence as a board member, and saw that I was some place I had no place being, don't you see?"

Any suspicions that the Colonel was disgruntled were dispelled in September, when the company scheduled the opening of its new headquarters building to coincide with the Colonel's eightieth birthday. A huge crowd was on hand for the occasion. The Colonel was the star of the show. And to ice the cake, his office was the first one a visitor would see upon entering the building, just to the left of the main entrance. It was an extremely neat, uncluttered, somber office, primly furnished, with only a few family portraits on the wall, a far cry from his Shelbyville mare's nest.

The Colonel, mingling with the crowd, spotted a delegation from Corbin, and went over to speak to Roy Houser, of the chamber of commerce.

"Look at this, Roy," he said. "What do you think of a goddam thing like this?"

"What's wrong with it?" asked the astounded Houser. "Don't you like it?"

"It ain't like or not like," snorted the Colonel. "It's just somebody looking for ways to spend money. A bunch of young punks spent all this money just on an office. I tell you, Roy, they'll go broke, sure as hell."

But in what he called "my birthday boy speech," he was more gracious. After a procession of congratulatory telegrams, flowery speeches, and gushing references to "our goodwill ambassador," the Colonel got up and declared: "That sounded almost as bad as an obituary meeting. Still," he added, "I guess it's nice to hear good things said about you instead of hearing the real record."

At eighty, the Colonel gave no indication that he intended to slow down, or wanted to. He was still full of plans, always had some new project underway, often to the dismay of company attorneys who had to remind him repeatedly that he could not start, take part in, or franchise businesses using his famous image, name, or slogan without company approval. He had become actively involved in a fosterchild program in which he provided support for homeless or troubled children; in time he would have eighty-five of them under his care. He assured everyone at his birthday party that "I've got at least twenty more of these [birthdays] left in me. I'll hit one hundred easy. Take me that long to do the things I've got on the fire right now."

But to those close to him, it was evident that time was taking its toll. He was named "Poster Boy of the Year" by the National Arthritis Foundation, and cheerfully posed for the posters heralding its annual fund drive. But his own arthritis was becoming more painful. He tried a variety of cures, including hot-wax baths for his hands. Each one seemed to help for a while, but the pain and stiffness always returned.

It irritated him. He hated to feel time taking its toll on his body, which had always been so tough and resilient. In spirit, he still felt vigorous, energetic, interested in living, and capable of enjoying it. But his body was not responding as it had. He hurt more in the morning. It took him longer to get going. He found it handy to use a cane (and the day he began using one, he began receiving dozens from admirers). His hip hurt him, and Claudia noticed that he had begun to lean a bit to the left when he walked. He had to have his glasses changed for stronger lenses. His doctor suggested that he think about getting a chauffeur. The thought shook him; he had always driven himself, and prided himself on being a good driver, capable of long, fast hours behind the wheel.

The thought of aging, more than the thought of dying, perplexed the Colonel. He insisted that he was "ready to go" if the Lord called him, but he wasn't. He wanted not only to live, but to enjoy it, and he wondered, to himself and to others, why it was that the body had to deteriorate with age, why it gradually lost its regenerative, recuperative power, why one day the cells, given the same foods, liquid, and use as before, no longer restored and revived the tissues, why eyesight dimmed and blurred, why joints swelled and stiffened.

But he still kept up a pace. A few weeks before his birthday, he and Claudia took off for a trip to Egypt, Russia, and the Holy Land. He didn't think much of Russia; the food was bad, the service was bad, and the people looked at him strangely. Egypt fascinated him. But it was the Holy Land that made the deepest impression. On September 3, 1970, both he and Claudia were baptized in the Jordan River.

It was the realization of an old dream, and his glowing, almost awed accounts of the event upon his return home showed its deep emotional impact. Regardless of his tongue and temper, Harland Sanders had always been a basically religious man. His was not a sophisticated or scholarly religion. He believed in the Bible, but seldom read or studied it, his Christianity springing from faith and total acceptance of the traditional tenets of right and wrong rather than an intellectual examination of Scripture. Sin, damnation, salvation—that was enough. He became friends with evangelists Billy Graham and Jerry Falwell. And he firmly believed "like the Book says," that he would go to heaven or hell when he died, according to the way the Lord added up his account.

So there was more than mere symbolism in his baptism in the Jordan waters. To Claudia it seemed a good and proper thing to do, but Harland did not question or doubt that the waters of baptism washed away the stain of sin. His tour of Jerusalem, and the walk along the path taken by Christ to the torture ground of Golgotha was not just a moving, but a cleansing experience.

As he grew older, the Colonel apparently felt an increasing need for religion and the forgiveness it offered. He was acutely aware of sin and the torments it brought, and at times the Colonel thought guiltily about the transgressions of Harland. He had not always been a moral man. His temper had led him into dozens of fights, and he had even wounded a man. He fretted constantly about his coarse language (but did nothing to correct it). During his Corbin years, he had acquired a reputation as a womanizer. (This, as Ona May Barbati said, was understandable. "The Colonel was an emotional, loving man, and the sex drive is a natural part of life, especially for men like that, and though I liked her, I have to say that Josephine was not a warm woman. She just didn't like sex and that was all there was to it. You couldn't blame him.")

But his had been a boyhood upbringing of Midwestern puritanism. It was in the nature of things to lust, sin, and suffer. He took unusual comfort from being washed in the waters of the Jordan River.

Now, six days later, he was back home basking in the limelight, as Louisville observed Colonel Sanders Day in honor of his eightieth birthday with the opening of the company's new office building. For him, 1970 proved to be a very good year.

13

What made Colonel Sanders run? Friends, watching him hurry from one event to the next, his black cane tapping restlessly as if in rhythm to the relentless tempo of his life, often wondered why he seemed so unsatisfied, so unwilling to rest a little and enjoy the later years of his life.

By 1971, his empire (or, if not exactly his, the empire built on his idea and nurtured on his image) had spread into forty-eight countries, with more than three thousand outlets. He was many times a millionaire, and more than three hundred others who had followed him into Kentucky Fried Chicken were, too. He was happily married. He was popular, and he talked with the mighty and powerful. His office walls showed pictures of him with people ranging from TV personalities to Presidents. What more could he want?

Not money. He and Claudia lived simply. When they were home, they did their own cooking. He usually prepared the meat. She fixed the vegetables. They liked to putter around the kitchen or watch television, talking little, often paying little apparent attention to each other, in the manner of people long-married. His temper flared when he felt he was not being paid enough, but his accountant had warned him that if he should die suddenly, the government would take most of his money in inheritance taxes, and he was busily giving it away against this horrible possibility.

He took no pleasure from leisure; in fact, he opposed the very idea. Called to Washington in the fall of 1971 to appear before a House subcommittee on the problems of aging, he warned the members that, "If you want to keep from having problems about getting old, for God's sake don't think about retiring. It's the worst mistake a man can make. It'll kill you quicker'n anything. Even if we can afford to, we should not rely on loafing." And he repeated his old slogan: "A man will rust out quicker than he will wear out."

"People should keep an eye on what's coming up, not what's slipping by," he said. "Senior citizens may lack physical strength and agility, but they are rich in added perspectives, and these late years are a crown to wear." (Rather graceful English for a man who pretended an inability to speak proper grammar.)

When Liberal Congresswoman Bella Abzug suggested that there might be a need for improved social programs, such as rent supplements and food payments for older citizens less able than the Colonel, he would have none of it.

"We're too prone to lean on someone else," he told her quietly. "Senior citizens should get out of bed and strike out on their own instead of looking for the dole." Later, he warned against the welfare system: "It's a sin to put a man on welfare if he isn't helpless. You don't do a man any favor by making him a bum, giving him a living for doing nothing. That rots a man inside."

He meant it. Inactivity made him uneasy. He sold his Shelbyville restaurant to Fred Settles and his wife Tommy, a former waitress (but kept a fatherly eye on it, watching the help and checking out the kitchen every time he went in to eat). He became a major investor in the Cape Codder, a seafood chain based in Kentucky. He talked about franchising a restaurant chain of his own, specializing in home cooking like the fare he had served at his Shelbyville restaurant. After the restaurant was sold, he and Claudia moved to Louisville (though the Colonel had always insisted that he did not like to live in a big town) and bought a comfortable-looking redbrick home in suburban Hurstbourne.

Watching him eat at the Shelbyville restaurant was like watching the return of a conquering hero. Coming into the dining room he always made a grand entrance, standing for a moment in the doorway, glancing imperiously around the room until people noticed him. The waitresses always fussed and fluttered around him—"Good evening, Colonel," "How're you this evening, Colonel?" "Where'd you like to sit, Colonel?" He would smile benevolently as they led him to a table.

But after he ordered, he would glance restlessly around the room and his fingers would drum the table. He needed involvement. He wanted an audience, and usually got one. Sooner or later, a young couple would approach, apologizing for bothering him, just wanting to say hello so they could tell the folks back home. And then, as if the footlights had come up, he would rise, bowing to "this charming lady" with a grand flourish, the admiration in their eyes food for his ego.

His ego was given another treat when, in the summer of 1971, he was invited back to "the place where it all started" to be Corbin's "Citizen of the Year." He was returning in triumph not only to the place where he had pumped gas and wiped windshields, but to the place where, when he engaged in a gunfight, the local papers identified him as "H. D. Saunders." He was returning not just to the plaudits of well-wishers, but to the praise of those who had ridiculed his "wild chicken scheme." He savored the moment.

"He enjoyed it," said Roy Houser of the chamber of commerce. "He hadn't forgotten anybody, called everybody by name. That was like him. He would take a dislike to a man just by looking at him. But if he liked you, he would borrow money to help you."

"There was an element of tragedy in the relationship between Sanders and Corbin," said Jim Lee Crawford, publisher of the Corbin *Times-Tribune*. "He wasn't a very good businessman, you know. Too impulsive. Spent money like crazy or gave it away. He always had to drive that big white Cadillac, go to Florida every year, even if he was up to his neck in debt. He was rough on his employees, but they found him a soft touch if they were down on their luck.

"When he sold out, he still owed a lot of money around town, and people who had seen him jump from one scheme to another and throw his money around were just naturally reluctant to take him seriously and invest with him when he started franchising. So later, when he became successful, the people of Corbin were left out. They could have been part of it."

But now the people of Corbin were cordial to the Colonel, and he to them, declaring in a graceful speech that he remembered his years in Corbin as happy ones. He seemed pleased with the occasion, posed for pictures in front of his old restaurant, and on his way back to Shelbyville grumbled about what John Brown was doing to the company.

What Brown was doing was tightening ship. He was also thinking about leaving it. Like the Colonel, he was a restless man who liked the excitement of big plans, actions, decisions, and now he found himself involved in what he considered the dull routine of management. He wanted a change. He began to fret that he spent too little time at home with his children, John Young III, Eleanor, and Sandra. His involvement with the Kentucky Colonels basketball team had not been satisfying; he felt that the community had not supported the team as he had expected, and was relieved finally to sell his interest in it. The fish and chips investment had turned sour. He had transferred the roast beef outlets to the Hungry Hermit Restaurants, six of which the company had bought, along with two pancake houses. The Hermit and pancake houses, though, were making nice profits.

Brown was rumored to be spending a lot of time in Las Vegas, where he was said to win and lose huge sums. "Actually," he said, "I don't do much gambling anymore; the fun has gone out of it. Money is what makes gambling fun. When I was hustling, trying to get a start, $500 was a lot of money, and winning $500 was exciting. There's no real excitement in it any more. What do I need with another $500?"

No one around KFC headquarters was really surprised when, in March 1971, Brown opened talks with officials of Heublein, Inc., producer of packaged foods and premixed drinks, about a possible merger of the two firms. Ten days later, the talks were called off without explanation. A week later, they started again, and on April 10, Heublein announced from its home offices in Hartford, Connecticut, a merger under which each share of KFC stock would be exchanged for .55 shares of Heublein stock. KFC directors accepted the Heublein offer on May 7. The stockholders approved it on May 10.

At the time, Brown was president, chief executive officer, and chairman of the KFC board. Under the merger, he remained president and board chairman of KFC for five years, with a salary of $100,000 a year for three years, and $50,000 a year for the last two. He, Pete Harman, and the Colonel would sit on the board of Heublein.

An era had ended. The days of the "lean, hungry," daring young men were over. The era of the cool corporate executive, with his eye on orderly structure and a good bottom line, was beginning. They would pose problems for the Colonel, and he would present problems for them.

Brown announced the merger with evident relief. It was widely rumored that he wanted to be free to go into politics, and when he resigned as president within two months, to be succeeded by Barry Rowles, the rumors grew hotter. The Colonel shrugged off the whole thing, saying it made no difference to him.

As a matter of fact, it made a considerable difference. The new officers knew little about the company history, about the Colonel or his achievements, and as long as he did his public relations job and appeared on the TV commercials, they tended not to care greatly. Some didn't see why he was needed around at all. John Brown did and he eventually showed them.

"The Heublein people didn't really understand or appreciate the Colonel," he said. "They were corporate people. They didn't respect what he had done. Didn't know. They were going to cut him out of their ads. They told me that they hadn't made up their minds whether they were going to use the Colonel or not.

"You have to give the man credit. He had a good, going company. It was no little one-man joke. He had a good base, a good system. He was making good money. These house ads said that when we took over it was a struggling little operation. It was no such thing. It was ready to bust out. We took what he had done and within six years went international all because of him. It was all based on him. He was the difference between us and the other food companies. They couldn't understand that."

The Colonel thought less of the new officers than they thought of him. When Mike Miles came in as senior vice-president of marketing in July 1971, the Colonel apparently took one look at him and decided he had no use for him.

"He simply didn't like me," said Miles. "I didn't have any grease burns on my arms. In the Colonel's view, I didn't know anything about the business. One of the first things he ever said to me was, 'How many pots of chicken you ever cooked, boy?' The answer was none, and he was sensitive to that. He liked people who understood the business, and he was right. It was absolutely necessary for me to get into the stores and learn their operation. By the time I left, I would say I was fairly high on his enemies list. Barry [Rowles, first president under Heublein] took the heat, and they didn't get along too well, either.

"But when I returned in 1977 as KFC board chairman, the Colonel came to my office and said, 'Mr. Miles, I have learned a lot of things while you were gone, and I assume you have learned a lot of things, and if I'm right and we're both smarter, we should get along fine.' I gave him a big hug, and from that day on we got along fine."

But the years with Rowles were not easy ones for the Colonel. John Brown, during his last months as head of KFC, had had a disagreement with Pat Gorman, and Gorman had quit. To soften the blow, Brown offered to sell him the Colonel's old Sanders Cafe in Corbin at a very low price, and Gorman grabbed it.

("That was typical of John," said John Cox, vice-president in charge of public relations. "If he had to fire somebody, he'd give him a break on a franchise or something. He wasn't nearly as tough as he tried to pretend.")

Gorman went down to Corbin and found the place in terrible shape. Jack Clare was managing it, and the roof leaked so badly he had to cook in a raincoat. The motel had been so badly damaged by fire it had to be torn down. Gorman took the place and fixed it up, reopening with a splash of advertising and publicity. He got a big boost when, with the help of history buff Frank Rankin, he got Lieutenant Governor (later Governor) Julian Carroll to designate the restaurant a historic site, and place a state historical marker at the roadside in front of the building. The Colonel, Rowles, and a raft of state and local dignitaries came for the dedication of the marker and the opening of the new cafe. Gorman soon sold it. He made a killing.

On the way back to Louisville, the Colonel and Rowles snapped and needled each other.

"It was just a case of two different types," said Cox. "The Colonel started out liking Rowles, but ended up despising him. The next year, for his birthday, I gave him a dart board, with Barry's picture silk-screened on it. He got a kick out of that."

The Colonel didn't like his new home in Hurstbourne any

more than he liked the new officers at KFC. "I didn't like living that close to people," he said. "Every time I looked out my back window, I could see into everybody's yard." At one point, an awning salesman called on the Colonel, who ordered red-and-white-striped awnings for the house. His neighbors were not exactly crazy about the innovation, which violated the rather rigid restrictions of the conservative suburb. The Colonel decided that he wanted to move. He said nothing about his plans to Claudia, who liked living in Louisville. Officials at KFC gave them a small greenhouse, thinking that would make the Colonel feel more at home, and give him a hobby. He scoffed at it as a "gadget." "Can't raise anything in a damn gadget like that," he later told John Brown.

Though John still maintained an interest in Kentucky Fried Chicken, and the Colonel was still, under the original contract, a public relations man and goodwill ambassador for the company, he and Brown saw little of each other during the first part of 1971. The Colonel and Claudia had been traveling a lot, and the Colonel, who always liked to eat when he got to cities famous for their food, had put on weight. The doctor told him to take some off.

"He was always overweight," says Brown. "Overweight by forty, fifty pounds, too, the only old, fat man since Winston Churchill who could go as hard as he did. But he was strong as a bull. Always felt good, or said he did, always had something to look forward to, perfect proof that the key to longevity is being active and interested."

The Colonel had heard of a rice diet being offered at Duke University at Durham, North Carolina, and he and Claudia went down to try it. They had a fine time; he lost twenty pounds and came home declaring that his arthritis had "eased up on me."

During his first week under the Duke treatment, the Colonel complained to his nurses that his job was wearing him out, that he had to travel too much, and that he couldn't keep up the pace at his age. The nurses, not knowing that this was his standard way of "blowing off steam," took him very seriously, and some of them became worried about him. Just before he left, his head nurse said to him, "Colonel, you are right. You don't need that job and all that work. You ought to quit and take it easy."

"Quit?" he asked in astonishment. "Quit work? What in hell would I do? I'd die!"

Of course, he didn't quit. He bought a new home. And in a most peculiar way. Being the Colonel, he couldn't just go to a realtor and ask if he had any small farms listed. He had to ask Paul Johnson, a baker in Shelbyville, who told him that Ed Morris, out on Lagrange Road, had moved across the road, and that his old dairy farm might be for sale. The Colonel drove out to see Morris, found him building a modern brick home on his new property, and asked him if he wanted to sell the new house instead of the farm. Morris said no, that he and his family had planned it and were looking forward to moving in. Whereupon the Colonel offered him so much money he couldn't refuse.

Not everyone was overjoyed at this transaction. Particularly Claudia.

"I liked living in Hurstbourne," she said. "He never said anything to me about not liking it. First thing I knew, he just announced that he had bought this place from Ed Morris. Morris had thirty-two acres and this new house that he hadn't even finished. But he moved in in December, and he was still working on it when he sold it to H.D. [the Colonel] in May.

" 'Well,' the Colonel said to him, 'I'll give you two acres next door for you to build on, and you all can just stay here in the house till you get it built, and we'll just live down in the basement, plenty of room down there.' So Ed stayed in the house for seven months till he got his house finished, and we stayed in the basement. Why, I don't know. We didn't need to get out of the house we had in Hurstbourne, but he was just busting to get away and get over here. He said, oh, it was fun living in the basement. Well, maybe it was fun for him because he wasn't ever there, being on the road all the time. I didn't think it was so fun."

The Colonel was pleased with his new home, but there was at least one thing about which he was not pleased. His eyesight was measurably worse, so much so that his doctors practically forbade him to drive, and told him to get a driver. He hesitated for months, until Claudia and officials at KFC insisted on it. He then hired what proved to be a succession of drivers, all of whom either quit or were fired after a few months. As in everything else, the Colonel wanted his car driven where, when, and—most important—how he ordered. He did not want a driver arguing with him, even if he was only pointing out that what the Colonel wanted to do was in obvious violation of traffic laws. As Maureen McGuire had found years before, "It just didn't do to cross him."

He finally hired Dick Miller, a tall, slender, dark-haired, bespectacled Shelby County millworker who found that "there was a right way, a wrong way, and the Colonel's way of doing things. He wasn't always right, but if you wanted to get along with him, you made out he was right. I let him do what he wanted to, and no argument out of me. He wanted to drive, I let him drive. I said to him, 'It's your car.'"

But, as became apparent early in 1972, more than failing eyesight was bothering the Colonel. He had never cared for doctors. When he was well and strong, as he had been most of his life, or when he sought cures from doctors who could give him at best only temporary relief from the symptoms of time's toll, the Colonel tended to be scornful of the whole field of medicine. "Quacks," he would snort. When he had split his scalp in the collapse of the bridge at Camp Nelson, he had refused to let anyone call a doctor. "I can do as much as those bloodsuckers," he had snarled, "and it won't cost me half of what I've got."

Yet he was an easy mark for every quack cure that came down the pike. During his eighties, he tried copper bracelets, megavitamins, hot soaks, hypobaric oxygen tanks, and herbal medicines. His hope flared anew with each report of a new arthritis cure or rumors of hormones that would lessen the natural deterioration of the body. But he was afraid of doctors, probably because he knew that they would tell him the truth, and he feared the truth. He had a horror of senility, of having his brain grow dim and foggy. And sometimes he let these vague fears lead him to ridiculous abuse of his aging body. It was such an occasion that led him, in the spring of 1972, to Louisville's Dr. Angelo Ciliberti, who would become his friend, as well as his physician, for the rest of his life.

"I had been a professor at the University of Louisville med school and was just going into practice when Charlie—Dr. Charles—Pearce called and asked me to see this Colonel Sanders, said it was an emergency. I said, 'All right,' and he came in, and I could hardly believe it. He had been sick for several days, but he had this commercial appointment in Chicago, and had gone through with it, and all the time obviously a sick man in his eighties. He was running a fever of 103, 104, having severe chills, terribly fatigued. I said to him, 'What in the world are you doing? Why didn't you stop work?' And he said he had this responsibility, and all these people depending on him, so he would work until the chill or fever hit him, and then lie down a while until it passed, and then start work again. He was like that, I found. He always felt his responsibilities very keenly.

"He was very sick. He had a bad urinary tract infection. I insisted on hospitalizing him, and it was then, after we had given him tests, that we picked up the fact that he was diabetic. He also had an enlarged prostate and couldn't clear his bladder. A very sick man. Well, we got the infection under control, and got the fever down, and let him go home for a few days before surgery for the prostate. And we began treating him for the diabetes; it was of a type that could be controlled by diet. And during that time, we began feeling each other out. He was always feeling out people, seeing how they responded to him.

"He came back in for the surgery, and the first day after the operation I went in to see him and there he was walking up and down the hall. That was the fantastic thing about this man. I don't mean that he was sitting up in his room, as we encourage them to do, or walking around his bed. He was walking up and down the hall, just hours after surgery on his prostate.

"You couldn't stop him; he was going to do what he wanted to do the minute you were gone. On the third day, I think it was, he said he had to go out the next day to a Salvation Army dedication; he had given money for a building or something, and he wanted to be there. And I said, 'No way! There's just no way I'm going along with you on this, Colonel.' And he grumbled something and went on back to bed. The next day, a Sunday, I got a call from the hospital, and they said he had gotten up, dressed, and walked out, saying he had to go to this Salvation Army thing and would be back that night. And he came back. I gave him hell, but I could see it was making no impression. He wasn't going to listen to any damned doctor. I began to realize the kind of man I had on my hands.

"After that, I saw him sporadically, usually because of his diabetes, which was no big problem, and we finally got a bit closer. And a couple of years later, he said to me, 'Tell you what I'm going to do; I'm going to give you a contract. I want you to keep me alive till I'm ninety.' And I said, 'Okay. I'll keep you alive till you're ninety.' It became a sort of joke.

"He was a fascinating man. Exasperating, too. He would buy the craziest schemes. Later on, when he took that trip to the Orient, I got this call, I think it was from Thailand, and he had found this doctor who had a wonderful herb medicine that would keep him young. I got the guy on the phone, but he spoke very poor English. I got the Colonel back on the line and told him, 'Colonel, look around you. Don't you see old people? If this stuff worked, would they be old? Do me a favor. Bring this stuff home and let's analyze it and if it won't hurt you, you can take it.' So he did, but by the time he got home he'd forgotten about it.

"He'd say to me, 'What do you know about this hypobaric oxygen?' I said, 'What do you want it to accomplish?' And he said he just wanted to keep his mind clear. Said he didn't want to get to be a damned old fool.

"He went down to Birmingham later to be in some sort of parade. He rode with Governor George Wallace, and was telling him about his eye problems, and Wallace talked him into going to the University of Alabama Medical School for examination. The first thing I knew, he was calling me, telling me he was considering this operation. They had fine doctors there, of course, and this one doctor had discovered that he had this murmur in an artery in his neck, indicating a formation of plaque in the artery, which, if it broke loose, could cause a stroke, and they were considering an operation. I talked to the doctor, who agreed that if the Colonel was going to be operated on, it would be better if he came home, where he would be close to his own people and to doctors familiar with him. We never did the operation. I didn't think it was going to help his eyesight enough to justify the risk. But there was always something like that."

None of this was slowing the Colonel down much, and while he was dashing around the country in his duties for KFC, John Brown was preparing to set off in new directions. As soon as he was free of his obligations to Kentucky Fried Chicken, he formed a group and bought Lum's, a chain of 52 company-owned and 260 franchised restaurants selling hot dogs, roast beef, and beer. John expanded the menu, changed the decor, and four months later sold the company-owned restaurants to Riviana Foods, Inc., for $6 million. He later sold the franchised Lum's for $11 million, not a bad return considering he had paid $4 million for the bunch.

But he was still interested in politics and in 1971 had been elected chairman of the Democratic Party's Young Leadership Council. Meeting with party leaders, he heard them complaining about the party debt of $9 million, and suggested that they authorize him to conduct a nationwide telethon to raise some money to pay off the debt. Most party bigwigs were skeptical, but Brown persuaded a host of entertainment figures to appear on the show, told his listeners they could pay by credit card, and asked all Democrats to come to the aid of their party. He raised $5 million—not enough to pay the entire debt, but

enough to keep the bill collector from the door—and in the
process earned the respect and gratitude of the party leaders.

When the Democrats convened in Miami in 1972 to nomi-
nate a candidate for President, Brown had another idea, this
one involving the Colonel. The Colonel was, to say the least,
unenthusiastic, but John wheedled and coaxed and finally persuaded him to go along. John's proposal to the Democratic
National Committee seemed simple enough. He would give
each of the delegates, officials, and newsmen a box luncheon of
Kentucky Fried Chicken, free of charge, and give the committee a donation of $3,500 for the privilege of making this good-
will gesture. The committee said, "Go ahead."

It proved to be one of the greatest coups in television history. With the cameras of all three major networks and hundreds of news photographers grinding and clicking, ten thousand people broke out brightly painted, red-and-white-striped
boxes of Kentucky Fried Chicken. For hours, the nation was
treated to the spectacle of delegates devouring the chicken,
and the sight of the distinctive boxes littering the floor and
aisles for hours afterward. For $3,500, Brown had gotten more
than a million dollars' worth of advertising.

But it was the Colonel who stole the show. Delegates stood
and cheered as he entered the hall, just after the free chicken
had been handed out. Security men had to usher him through
the admiring crowd. Democratic dignitaries from presidential
hopefuls to delegates from Podunk came up to shake his hand.
He was given a thunderous ovation when he was called to the
podium for official introduction.

It was a smash hit. A few days later, Brown's name began to
be heard as a possible running mate for the Democratic nominee, George McGovern. A month later, KFC again benefited
from the publicity coup when the American Party, holding its
convention in Louisville, demanded equal treatment with the
Democrats and free lunches of Kentucky Fried Chicken. But
the Democrats claimed Brown and the Colonel as their own.

A week later, the Colonel came out with a public endorse-
ment of Richard Nixon, the Republican nominee.

14

Howls of anguish went up from the embattled Democrats. It was as though Robert E. Lee had sold out to the Union. And no one was more embarrassed than John Y. Brown, Jr. While his plans were vague, it was obvious that he had political ambitions, and whatever future he had clearly lay in the Democratic Party. But Brown had not gotten where he was by being unable to control his emotions.

In the Colonel's letter to Brown and Massey in November 1964, following his sale of the company, the Colonel had assured them that any criticism he, the Colonel, had would be made in private. That assurance had not lasted long. In the intervening years, the Colonel had lambasted Brown and Jack Massey loudly and publicly for "doing me out of my stock." He told a Chicago reporter that the men who had bought him out were "a bunch of sharpies." When Brown finally ran for office (for governor in 1979), the Colonel opposed him in the primary election, and denounced him at a fund-raising dinner for an opponent, Dr. Harvey Sloane.

If any of this angered Brown, he gave no sign. He was too much the old poker player to let impatience muddy his relations with a man so important to him. The Colonel's outbursts usually brought from him no more than a smile and the opinion that, "The old man's just blowing off steam." When the Colonel supported Richard Nixon for President, Brown would say only that, "The Colonel is one of a kind. He makes up his own mind, even when he makes it up wrong."

And not only did the Colonel make up his mind, he spoke it, often to the dismay of KFC public relations men. While on a business trip to Chicago during the first week of December 1972, he remarked casually to a reporter that the gravy served at most Kentucky Fried Chicken stores "tastes like wallpaper paste." He went on to describe the various sins of the company, adding, "I haven't liked that gravy for years."

He then rubbed more salt into Democratic wounds by describing his appearance at the Miami convention as "something I didn't want to do."

"I didn't want to go down there with that class of people," he sniffed. "But they paid me $75,000 [his salary at the time] and it was on prime time, so I went. But I'm sorry about it." This could not have been very soothing to John Brown, who had just been chosen chairman of the Jefferson-Jackson Day dinner, with which Kentucky Democrats hoped to revive sagging party spirits.

Nor did the Colonel stop there. Sure, he liked fried chicken, he said. But "I'd run my legs off for a Limburger on rye. You just can't get a decent Limburger on rye in Kentucky."

Brown made no comment. The public relations office at KFC said simply, "The Colonel is the Colonel. Whatever the Colonel wants to say, the Colonel can say." This was in itself pretty good evidence that KFC officials had realized the importance of the Colonel and his image to the future of Kentucky Fried Chicken, a considerable change from their attitude a few months earlier when they had taken over the company and had considered dropping the Colonel out of their promotion efforts altogether.

John Brown's tolerance for the Colonel's crotchety conduct had long been attributed to the fact that John needed to keep the Colonel happy and working. As the Colonel's Nicholasville friend, Albert McDowell, said, "John and the Colonel needed each other. Neither could have made it alone. But only John realized it."

But now John no longer needed the Colonel's services, and his patience and understanding can only be attributed to his sincere regard and affection for "the old man."

"The Colonel harbored these totally groundless grudges against John Y.," said John Cox, former KFC public relations director. "But John never showed any animosity toward the Colonel. I really think he loved the old man, and was patient with him no matter how provoked he became, and he must have been mighty provoked at the time. Not just because he is a cool customer and doesn't get upset when his money is at stake, but because he loved the Colonel, and respected him for what he had done, and wanted to see him happy. Nobody appreciates how much John did to keep that guy happy, though I think that in the end the Colonel realized how much John had done, and how much the gentleman he had been."

One trouble with being the Colonel, or being responsible for the Colonel's remarks, lay in the fact that the Colonel was a candid, outspoken man who lived in a goldfish bowl and never knew when his most casual private remark would be blown into an embarrassing news story. Working for the March of Dimes, one of his favorite charities, he had to travel from one city to another, making several personal appearances in a single day. It was a grueling routine, for him and for the young public relations man assigned to him by KFC.

Once, they had had no lunch, and had only minutes to get to a TV appointment. The Colonel ordered the driver to pull up to a hamburger stand, where he ordered a sandwich and milk. But, unknown to him, a TV camera crew was following him, and was soon busily filming the sight of the daddy of chicken eating in a hamburger shop. The poor PR man could see his job going glimmering, but the Colonel, seeing his anguish, hastened to explain to the TV men that he was just checking out the opposition, and eating not a hamburger but an egg sandwich which, as he pointed out, was the closest thing you could get to chicken in a place like that.

The incident showed that the old boy could still think on his feet. It also showed his kindness for the young PR man. But the Colonel was eighty-three, and the pressure of travel and constant public appearances was taking its toll. During the first week of July, he began to complain of stomach pains, and when they persisted, Dr. Ciliberti insisted that he enter the hospital for tests.

"He was always constipated," said Dr. Ciliberti. "And we have this thing in our profession that if a man is having trouble with his colon, we have to get a barium enema and X-ray him. So we did, and this barium enema showed this large polyp, tumor, extending from the inside of the colon. We reviewed it, got a couple of others to review it, and decided to get a repeat barium enema, this one out at Suburban Hospital. It showed the same polyp. It was big and it was suspicious-looking. So we showed him the X rays and explained that it had to be taken out so we could be sure it wasn't cancer of the colon.

"Well, he was just as casual as anything. 'Sure, sure.' So the surgeon goes in, and they study him, and there's no damned polyp. He calls me, and he says, 'Ange, I saw the X rays, and we've studied him thoroughly, and there just isn't any polyp, that's all.' And I thought: God! Here we've subjected him to surgery, and didn't take anything out. I could just hear him. So the next day I went in, the day after surgery, and here he is walking up and down the hall again, and I've really got my hat in my hand, you know, had to tell him we operated for nothing. I said, 'Jesus, Colonel, I hate to tell you this, but we opened you up and didn't find anything.' And he said, 'Hell, I knew you wouldn't. I know what happened.' I said, 'What do you mean?' And he told me that his minister had been in the night before, and they had prayed together, and the minister had laid his hands on him and told him that everything would be all right, and so he knew it would be.

"He said, 'Don't you believe that did it?' And I said, 'Hell no, I don't believe it. But if you do, I'm happy for you.' He was just as cool, as sure. What was it? It was a shadow on that X ray. Yes, even with two X rays. It was just too unscientific. But he believed it. And he never had any trouble with his colon again. Except for the usual constipation.

"That was mainly a matter of age; the stomach muscles lose their contracting power, sag. Actually, he took pretty good care of himself. Didn't drink or smoke, overate, but ate good food. Loved good food, and ate a pretty good diet. Slept well. He didn't turn and toss; he lay down and went to sleep. And John Cox always tried to arrange his schedule so that he could get a nap in the afternoon. He couldn't have kept up his pace otherwise."

Hospital spokesmen announced that the Colonel was recovering well from his surgery and would be back at work in six weeks. Less than three weeks later, he took off on a business trip to Canada, stopping in New York to have his portrait done by Norman Rockwell, whose paintings had for years graced the covers of *The Saturday Evening Post*. The portrait was commissioned by Win Shelton, now president of Collectramatic, which made machinery for the fast-food industry, including the all-important cooking-oil filter.

Still, though he protested that he felt "like a boy," some inner voice must have been reminding the Colonel of time's passage, for in April 1973, he picked out his grave site in Louisville's Cave Hill Cemetery. During the second week in April, he showed his chosen resting place, with that of Claudia close beside, to newsmen, pointing out the gray granite monument featuring four columns (suggesting the front of the KFC building) and, set in the center of the granite portico, a two-foot-high bronze bust, sculpted, he said proudly, by his daughter Margaret.

The Colonel made it plain to the accompanying newsmen

that he was not expecting to need the grave any time soon. "I'm just asking seventeen and a half more years," he said. "Then, when I'm one hundred, I'm going to turn it over to the young people."

Asked why he chose Cave Hill, rather than Corbin, where he lived for twenty-five years, or Shelbyville, then his home, or the Henryville cemetery near the place where he was born, the Colonel said, "Cave Hill is well kept. And it's close to home. And," he added finally, "it's a cemetery everybody will love." He was taking no chances on being stuck away somewhere and forgotten.

While he was picking out their grave site, Claudia was forming a partnership with a young Cincinnati designer named Harry Backus, and announced that they would soon begin franchising the Colonel's Lady Dinner House restaurants. The announcement prompted some worried conferences at KFC. "The Colonel's Lady" was getting a little too close for comfort.

No immediate action was taken, however, and relations between KFC and the Colonel seemed cordial enough when he and Claudia left in October for a promotional trip to Hong Kong, New Zealand, Australia, Japan, and China. The Colonel returned bubbling with details of his trip, and of his experiences in China where, he said, "They fix chicken different, but it's good." Customs, however, had held up his pressure cookers, and he had not had a chance to initiate the Chinese into the mysteries of preparing Kentucky Fried Chicken.

But back in Shelbyville, the Colonel was informed that Heublein was not happy about the proposal to franchise the Colonel's Lady Dinner Houses, and did not intend to allow it. The Colonel blew up. In January 1974, he and Claudia filed suit in U.S. district court against Heublein for $122 million.

The suit charged that Heublein was illegally interfering with Sanders' right to do business; that Heublein had used the Colonel's name and likeness promoting products with which the Colonel had never been connected; and that Heublein had fraudulently registered seventeen trademarks misrepresenting the source of the products and without the Colonel's consent.

Here, in brief, was the root cause of the Colonel's lingering resentment, first of John Brown and now of Heublein—their interpretation of the original contract. The Colonel had always maintained that he had sold only KFC, his name and image, and the terms "finger lickin' good" and "Tender and Tasty Colonel Sanders' Kentucky Fried Chicken," and the right to nothing more. No one ever knew whether he really believed this or whether, as John Brown said, he wished it so much he couldn't face the fact that it wasn't so.

Heublein moved cautiously. No one at headquarters relished the idea of a court fight with the Colonel, with all the publicity that would result. But the officers of KFC stuck to their guns, and on November 19, 1974, filed suit against the Colonel and Claudia, charging that the name "Claudia Sanders, the Colonel's Lady" and its variations violated KFC trademarks. The suit asked an injunction against use of the name, and asked that all advertising and promotional material being used in the effort to franchise the restaurants be destroyed.

"The company didn't want to punish the Colonel," said John Cox. "It just wanted to stop him. The reason they took such a hard line was that it was a precedent they couldn't permit. If he had been allowed to do that, then he or anyone could have gone off promoting and franchising anything carrying his name. It was the same reason we sold the motels; we didn't want to be in the motel business, but we didn't want anyone starting a chain with the name, so we sold them without the name."

John Brown had been watching the fight from the sidelines, and was unhappy about it. He began, in late summer of 1975, to see if he couldn't patch things up.

"My father and I dropped by to see him one night in Shelbyville," he recalled. "Just to say hello. I hadn't seen him in a while. He was all full of fire, at least on the surface. Said, 'I'm going to sue their ass.' I don't know whether he really thought he could win, but he seemed to be enjoying the fight. I said to him, 'Colonel, you've got to drop this. If this thing goes to court, I'll have to appear and testify against you, because we made that contract, you and I, and I know what's in it. And you're wrong. And you're going to lose. And I don't want to be in court against you. Now, I'm going to talk to the people over at the home office, if it's all right with you, and see what kind of settlement we can get. Is that all right with you?' And he looked at me a while, didn't bluster or cuss around, just said, 'Yeah, I guess so. Sure.'

"I went over to the Heublein people and told them his nose was out of joint, that he probably thought he hadn't gotten as much money as he should have, but that he was still valuable to them, that he was still their image, and that the suit would bring them a lot of hurtful publicity. I said, 'Tell me how far you'll go.' And they gave me some ground rules and I went back and got the Colonel and we went to New York and talked to his lawyer, and we sat right there and whacked out an agreement. I got the Colonel to agree. I got Heublein on the phone and they agreed. Then I walked in and threw down the contract and said, 'All right, Colonel; sign this damned thing,' and he did. Didn't even read it. Think of that! All that mess and fuss, just because nobody had taken the trouble to talk to him. Anyhow, he got $2 million over ten years, and Heublein got an agreement that he would quit trying to use the name. And that was about it.

"The old man was eighty-five that day. We got back on the plane and got back to Louisville for his birthday party. The company had about a thousand franchisees out at Executive Inn West. He had a big time. He and the Heublein people just as chummy. You just had to talk to him and work it out."

The suit, however, apparently hadn't changed the Colonel or his relations with the company. In October 1975, he visited a KFC store in Bowling Green, Kentucky, where he conducted his usual inspection of the premises and its offerings. He was not pleased. A week earlier, he had barged into a store in New York, where he scared the daylights out of the awestruck counterman by declaring that the food tasted like garbage. Seeing the face of the stricken employee, he softened, however, and added, "It's not your fault, son. That's the way they're running these places these days."

But on the Bowling Green visit, he was accompanied by Dan Kauffman, of the *Courier-Journal* in Louisville, who reported in great detail (and great glee) the Colonel's reaction to the fare.

"M-God!" the Colonel sputtered. "They buy tap water for fifteen or twenty cents a thousand gallons and then mix it with flour and starch and end up with wallpaper taste. That stuff is sludge." He added that, "There's no way you could get me to eat some of those potatoes." He also voiced strong objections to carrots in the coleslaw.

The owner of the store, not surprisingly, took exception to his remarks. In-house criticism, he said, was one thing. Statements in the press were something else. He promptly sued the Colonel for libel, demanding damages. When a lower court dismissed the suit, he appealed to the Kentucky Supreme Court, where the suit was decided in the Colonel's favor.

The company tried to keep a hands-off policy in such squabbles. But occasionally the Colonel's remarks made the people at headquarters wince, especially when reporters asked the company to comment. In both New York and Bowling Green, the Colonel had said, "You're just working for a company that doesn't know what it's doing. Too bad, because it gives you a bad reputation."

"We're very grateful to have the Colonel around," said hard-pressed Anthony Tortorici, assistant PR director. "He keeps us on our toes. But he is a purist. His standards were all right when he was operating a few stores. But we have over five thousand now, and that means more than ten thousand fry cooks of all ages and abilities. Raw chicken turns customers off, so we play it safe and fry it at a lower temperature for a longer time. And we think carrots add color and eye appeal to coleslaw. The Colonel has very high standards for his products, but we need wider parameters to operate in the real-life world. His gravy is fine, but it took a very fine cook to prepare it, and it took a long time. But I guarantee you that if you go back into that store (Bowling Green) you'll see a big improvement."

Not all of his statements were so inflammatory.

"They've been drifting away from my way for years," he said in response to the Tortorici statement. "But I think they're getting back to basics. About ninety-nine percent of the time, the chicken you buy today is as good as what I used to sell."

And behind his bluster, the Colonel did not want to end his relationship with the company. He liked being the image. He liked to make the personal appearances that he still made at a rate of about one hundred a year.

"If I had nothing to do when I get up, I'd go crazy," he told an interviewer as he approached his eighty-sixth birthday. "People ask me when I'm going to retire, and I tell them when the good Lord stops me." He had just returned from trips to Canada and Mexico. The company had just bought a huge hot-air balloon, shaped somewhat like a giant chicken, and he had insisted on being the first passenger.

The day following his eighty-sixth birthday party, he was scheduled to ride in the chicken balloon at the Kentucky State Fairgrounds. A big crowd was on hand to see him, snapping his picture and asking for autographs.

"I just love him," a woman squealed. "He's so cute!" The Colonel beamed.

"You nervous, Colonel?" a reporter asked him. The Colonel glared at him.

"I've never been nervous about anything," he replied. "I do just what I want to do." When the flight was canceled because of high winds, he was asked if he was disappointed.

"Just for the children," he said. "I've ridden it before. It would have been nice for them."

When asked about his health, the Colonel often seemed impatient.

"I don't worry about that," he snapped. "You start thinking you're sick and the first thing you know, you'll be sick. If you tell yourself you're doing all right, before you know it you'll forget what it was making you feel bad."

He was facing the prospect of a cataract operation. His eyesight had deteriorated to the point where he had to read the large-type edition of *Reader's Digest,* his favorite publication. But he still kept up with his mail, and kept two secretaries busy answering it and requests for autographed pictures.

The year 1976 had been a good one for him. In that year, the company announced British outlets had neared the hoped-for three hundred mark. Until 1973, Britons Harry Latham and Ray Allen had operated the British company under an agreement with the Colonel, but in that year they were sold to Heublein, though Latham continued as managing director of the British company.

"The thing that really set us off over here was the Colonel," said Latham. "When people saw him, the image offered the consistency of display backed up by the reassurance of the Colonel as a sort of father figure. Until then, most people thought he was just a trademark, that he didn't really exist."

The Colonel was impressed with the stores he visited in London, though he was surprised to find many of them stayed open all night, and scowled when he found them serving chips (french fries) instead of his trusted mashed potatoes.

During the last week in May 1977, the Colonel again traveled to Washington to testify before the House Select Subcommittee on Aging. Once more he told the lawmakers that mandatory retirement was a terrible thing.

"I'm dead against it," he declared. "I'm against retiring. The thing that keeps a man alive is having something to do. Sitting in a rocker never appealed to me. Golf or fishing isn't as much fun as working. You've got to stay alive to live. I'm eighty-six and going strong."

But the signs were growing to show that even the Colonel was mortal, that the old body was slowly wearing out. Shortly after returning home from Washington, he developed breathing problems. Again, he needed an operation. It was, as John Cox said, "unpleasant but not serious," and on the day he was released he sat in his Shelbyville home and joked with Claudia, Mildred, Margaret, and the inevitable newsman.

In September, as part of the ceremonies marking his eighty-seventh birthday, the Colonel dedicated KFC's new school of restaurant management, after which he spoke briefly to a crowd which included his old friend Pete Harman and other of his early franchisees, now all wealthy men. After that, he delighted the crowd by cooking and serving fried chicken, assuring the crowd that it was the genuine Kentucky Fried, with his own secret recipe of herbs and spices. The Colonel was charming. He made no criticism of anyone or anything.

Nineteen seventy-eight was a fairly quiet year for the Colonel and Claudia. He started a little garden behind his house on Highway 53 (but Dick Miller did most of the work). Occasionally, he saw John Y. Brown, who had been divorced from his wife Ellie in 1977, was serving as Kentucky's commissioner of economic development and thinking about getting more into politics.

On his eighty-eighth birthday, the Colonel and Claudia dedicated KFC's Colonel Sanders Museum, just off the lobby of the Louisville headquarters and only a few yards from the Colonel's office. One of the high points of the occasion was the unveiling of a bust of the Colonel sculpted by his daughter Margaret, now living in California.

After the unveiling, the Colonel walked around the museum, pointing out to friends some of the assembled memorabilia. There was the picture of the five-year-old Harland, with his mother, his sister Catherine, and his brother Clarence.

On the wall of the museum was a snapshot of Harland in his chef's hat, standing in his Corbin kitchen. At the touch of a button the visitor could see and hear a movie telling the story of his career. In a glass case, seeming small and awkward, was the first pressure cooker that he had ever used, with a big, shiny modern one beside it. On the walls were plaques, awards, and degrees that he, a sixth-grade dropout, had been given.

He had wanted to be someone, be remembered. Now he could be sure he would be. As he moved around the room, only an occasional twitch of his face betrayed the emotion he felt in moving among these reminders of yesteryears. Afterward, he made a short speech, expressing his gratitude. He warned that he was not through. "I've said it before, and I'll say it again: I'm going to keep on going until the day the Lord stops me."

But he slept most of the way back to Shelbyville.

15

Colonel Sanders had seen a lot of Derby Breakfasts, including quite a few given by various Kentucky governors in and around the official mansion in Frankfort. So had John Y. Brown, Jr., whose father had taken him to the mansion when he was a grade school boy. Neither man, as they faced the breakfast of 1979, was especially excited at the prospect of the food, which tends to run heavily to cheese grits and hot fruit. But both knew that the occasion was a handshaker's heaven. There are few places where you will find more grass-roots politicians, and both the Colonel and Brown wanted to take advantage of the fact. The Colonel was approaching his eighty-ninth birthday and was beginning to wonder how many more he would have. John Brown was running for governor of Kentucky.

Brown's unconventional, whirlwind, six-week campaign had surprised and shaken the state's traditional politicians. Before his unexpected announcement on March 27 that he was a candidate for the Democratic nomination for governor, most Kentucky politicos assumed that Brown was shifting his attention away from the Bluegrass State. He and Ellie were divorced. He had passed up a chance to run for the U. S. Senate. He had sold his Kentucky Colonels basketball team, and his stock in Kentucky Fried Chicken. He was spending increasing amounts of time in Miami, Boston, New York, and Las Vegas.

But on March 17 he had married Phyllis George, a former Miss America (1971) and the country's first big-time female TV sports commentator for the "NFL Today" pregame show and Sunday telecasts of National Football League games. When he was divorced in 1977, John said that the only other woman he had ever seen who interested him seriously was Phyllis George, whom he had seen only on TV screens. A few months after his divorce, he finally met the former Miss America while in New York, but their first date seems to have left no lasting impression on either. Later, Brown became convinced he had originally been right, and used his salesman's persuasion to win her.

They were married by Dr. Norman Vincent Peale, the preacher of the power of positive thinking, in his Marble Collegiate Church, on New York's Fifth Avenue, before a gathering of politicians, entertainers, and media stars. After a brief honeymoon, Brown announced that "we have decided" to run for governor of Kentucky. It seems likely the decision had actually been made some time before. By the time he filed for the race on March 27, Brown had had opinion samplers poll the state and design campaign strategy, which consisted primarily of a sales blitz.

Brown was certainly not unknown, but he entered a race in which other seasoned candidates had been running for over a year. Former state legislator Terry McBrayer, backed by Governor Julian Carroll, and former Louisville Mayor Dr. Harvey Sloane, were both considered good campaigners and the leading contenders for the nomination. Brown launched a barnstorming tour of the state, using planes and helicopters to make possible a dozen or more stops a day. He used his famous and photogenic bride to help him draw crowds. Employing interview techniques she had learned on TV, the new Mrs. Brown worked the crowds, prompting questions for John which he fielded with practiced ease, explaining that he was simply a successful businessman who wanted to bring business methods to Kentucky government, and use his proven talents to sell Kentucky to industrial investors across the country.

It worked. Brown nosed out Sloane by twenty-five thousand votes, and went on to defeat former Governor Louie Nunn (against whom he had previously decided not to run for the Senate) in the fall general election.

Colonel Sanders refused to endorse Brown or take part in his primary campaign, but came over to the Brown camp when the general election began. In fact, the race seemed to interest the Colonel very little. During August, despite the fact that he had not been feeling too well, he launched a twelve-city personal appearance tour for his old favorite, the March of Dimes, returning just in time to attend a huge party given by KFC in honor of his eighty-ninth birthday. As usual, the grind of being on the road was offset by the pleasure of talking to the children, and the Colonel said he had returned feeling better than when he had set out on the tour.

When John Brown won the governorship in a landslide, the Colonel was not among the throngs of celebrants in and around Louisville's Hyatt-Regency Hotel, where the election night victory party was held. He said later that he could see the proceedings just as well on television, and saw no reason to "go down there and let all those damn fools blow cigarette smoke on me and breathe liquor in my face." This was probably wise. He no longer enjoyed boisterous crowds. But it is also likely that he saw no possible pleasure in a victory in which he had played no part.

During the winter of 1979–80, the Colonel stayed home more than he had before, though he still went to the office for a while each weekday. There were always letters to sign, pictures to autograph, and he liked to speak to the people who came in to see the Sanders Museum. After an hour or so in the office, he seemed to get bored, and he would shuffle out, take the elevator to the second floor, and talk with John Cox, Janice Westerman, or Mike Miles.

"But he was slowing down," said his chauffeur, Dick Miller. "He didn't talk as much as he had, didn't cuss and complain as much. But he could still be ornery. I sometimes thought he was testing us to see who would put up with him and still love him.

"He got so he hated cigarettes more and more. Once he got so irritated with a lawyer who was smoking in his office that he reached over his desk and, to this guy's amazement, jerked the cigarette out of his mouth, jammed it against the wall, and said, 'There, goddammit!' "

"Some of his bluster was designed, I think, to cover his awareness of age," said John Cox. "He was by no means an ignorant man; he read everything, watched television. He had a horror of going blind; he had these cataracts, but the doctors had concluded that an operation for cataracts wouldn't improve his sight greatly, enough to justify the operation, so he never did it."

"It had gotten so we didn't travel so much," said Dick Miller. "But when we did, he still liked his Cadillac, always stayed in the best hotels, got limousine service at the airport, ate the finest foods. But when he was paying for it, he ate cheeseburgers. He didn't like picking up those checks."

The Colonel and Claudia observed Christmas quietly. Dozens of friends and relatives came by, and the Colonel seemed unusually glad to see them. Perhaps this was partly because he was now the sole surviving member of his childhood family. Clarence and Catherine, as well as his mother and father, were dead. After his shaky start, Clarence had settled down to become a stable, successful family man. Catherine had lived for several years in a Dayton, Ohio, nursing home, where she seemed quite happy.

A few years before her death, Catherine had bought a long, elaborately designed dress that she liked, specifying that she was to be buried in it. She sent it to the funeral home director she had chosen to conduct her burial and instructed him to keep it against the day she would need it. But in the meantime, she frequently received invitations to occasions calling for formal dress, and she would call the funeral director and ask if she could "borrow the dress" for the evening. She would wear it for the occasion, have it cleaned, and then send it back to the funeral home. The director got accustomed to "sending Catherine's dress to her." Then came the day when it was needed for the last time.

Even Josephine was gone, having died in Lexington in 1975 of congestive heart failure. The Colonel had been generous with her following their divorce, as had Margaret and Mildred, both of whom had prospered from their association with their father and his business.

Perhaps it was because of these deaths that, as 1980 began, the Colonel appeared to be putting his own house in order. Although he frequently declared, and with apparent sincerity, that money was not important to him, he was very sensitive about getting "what he had coming" to him. He made a good income; he received $125,000 a year from KFC for his public relations duties; he got another $100,000 a year from his Canadian company, and $100,000 from what company people call "the co-op," a board made up of ten franchisees and three company officials to supervise advertising for the entire chain. Every store pays one and a half percent of sales into the co-op, so that there can be coordination of advertising and agreement on policy. John Y. Brown had set it up.

But the Colonel hated to pay taxes, no matter how much he made. He considered taxes an evil and evidence of the evil side of government. He thought it was flatly wrong to make a man work all his life and then, when he finally made some money, take it away from him.

"That's why he arranged to give away as much as he could before he died," said John Cox. "And he did a pretty good job of it. He gave away most of the two million he got from Brown and Massey, and he set up that Canadian foundation to give all his Canadian profits to charity. He always said he wanted to provide for Claudia and make sure the government didn't get 'a goddam nickel' if he could help it."

Not that the Colonel was thinking about dying. Even during the blustery days of winter and early spring, he refused to stay home. He went to his office, he visited Kosair Children's Hospital, and he still averaged a trip a week on either company business or charitable fund raisers. If he was hurting particularly, he said nothing about it.

"I think it was then that I realized what an extremely proud man the Colonel was," one source said. "He took pride in his clothes—he would never wear a suit when it began getting shiny—in his car, in his appearance.

"But he hated to shave. It was hard to shave around the mustache and goatee, and I think it hurt his arthritic hands, so he would try to get away with shaving every other day. He was very proud of his masculinity; he didn't mind having it known that he had an eye for a pretty girl, and sometimes when he started telling stories about the old days, he'd hint that he'd had his days—or nights—with the women."

Still, as though impelled by premonition, several times that spring the Colonel drove to Louisville's Cave Hill Cemetery to inspect his grave site. Twice, he simply drove by, as though to make sure that the granite columns and bronze bust were still in place, but once he got out and, with the wind whipping his thinning white hair, walked up and down looking thoughtfully at his grave. Then with a vigorous nodding of his head, he returned to his car. "It's all right," he said absently, to no one in particular. "All right."

As the Kentucky Derby approached, the Colonel once more geared himself up for the festivities. He had done his duty in the past as parade marshal and as judge for the steamboat race, he decided, but he wanted to go to the traditional dinner given by the Loyal Order of Kentucky Colonels. Over the years, he had become not only the most famous of all colonels, but had taken a personal interest in the Loyal Order and its charities, and had consented to act as chairman of its charity campaign. It was too bad, he often said, that so many of the colonels felt it necessary to drink liquor and smoke those rotten-smelling goddam cigarettes, but they were a fine bunch of men. They did good work. He resolved to be more active in the Loyal Order in the future.

And, perhaps as his own way of apologizing, or coming as close to apology as Harland Sanders could come, he and Claudia drove to the Lexington home of Governor John Y. Brown, Jr., for the traditional Derby Breakfast. (A year earlier, a legislative committee had found the governor's mansion at Frankfort so in need of repairs and modernization that it was declared unsafe for the first family. So John and Phyllis simply moved their residence to the white Colonial home John had bought, together with seventeen acres of bluegrass land, just off Lexington's Tates Creek Pike. The name of the estate—Cave Hill—was not related in any way to Louisville's Cave Hill Cemetery, where the Colonel had chosen his grave site.)

Governor Brown bustled around the elderly white-haired man as though he were a favorite uncle, and gradually the Colonel began to unbend and turn on the charm, talking and joking.

"I think that toward the end, the Colonel realized how much John meant to him," said John Cox. "I know he thought that John was doing a good job of running the state."

With the Derby had come a stream of guests to the Shelbyville home, and Claudia and the Colonel were glad to see the familiar faces. The Colonel was in high, good spirits, but some of his old friends from early franchise days remarked that he seemed to have lost quite a bit of weight and looked tired. He did, and not without reason. He was pushing ninety. For thirty years, he had been plagued with arthritis. He had diabetes. He had weathered operations on his intestines and throat, and had suffered through kidney and bladder infections. And he had cataracts.

Yet, he insisted that he was as good as new. He had plans for a garden, for another tour for the March of Dimes. He had hopes for another trip to the Orient with Claudia. But the tough physique was beginning to slump. The famous face looked hollow-cheeked. A week after the Derby, he complained of chest pains. Dr. Ciliberti put him in the hospital. He had pneumonia.

"He was tired, as much as anything else," said the doctor. "He responded well to medication and rest, but about the time he was getting well, he said he had to get out, had to go to the KFC convention in Las Vegas. I don't know whether he suspected it might be his last one, but he was determined to go.

"I talked to John Cox, and he said they would let him appear about an hour a day, just to speak to the delegates and pose for pictures. They offered to fly me and my wife if I'd go to look after the Colonel. I said all right. They gave us the company jet; all the other executives took commercial flights so we could have it."

But in Las Vegas, the Colonel flatly refused to follow the easy schedule set up by John Cox. Instead, he got up at six every morning, went to all of the meetings, and then posed for hours for pictures with the delegates.

"It was crazy," said Ciliberti. "I couldn't do anything about it. Neither could Claudia. The guy was not just a workaholic. I think it had something to do with his traditional sense of values: a day's pay for a day's work. When I raised hell with him, he said, 'I'm getting good money from these people, and they're entitled to an honest day's work.'"

The Colonel enjoyed the Vegas convention tremendously. It was like a homecoming. All the old familiar faces were there, and he was clearly the hero of the occasion. People clamored for pictures with him. He was surrounded by well-wishers everywhere he went. But it had a price.

On June 8, the Colonel said that he "didn't feel too hot." It is likely, since he hated any kind of complaining, that he felt considerably worse than he admitted. Two days later, with Claudia and John Cox accompanying him, he entered Louisville's Jewish Hospital with pneumonia.

"You get a man in the hospital, you start running tests on him," said Dr. Ciliberti. "When we got the results of his blood tests, I took one look and began checking my records. His blood count had been so high, so good, and now it was very low. That was what made us suspicious. So we began making bone marrow tests, and that's when we found he had leukemia."

As usual, the Colonel was restless at being confined to a room, but submitted to the tests and seemed grateful for the opportunity to rest. Then, on the afternoon of June 10, Dr. Ciliberti, along with specialists and hospital staff doctors, came solemnly into his room and told him, gently but bluntly, that he had acute leukemia.

For a moment, the Colonel looked silently, thoughtfully, at the wall, then turned and asked, "Well, just how bad is that?"

The doctors explained that it was a form of cancer of the blood and of the blood-producing bone marrow of the body. Again, the Colonel hesitated, gazing out the window at the early summer day, the new green of the trees and grass. "Well," he said finally, "does anybody ever get over this?" The doctors admitted that not many people did. The information didn't seem to faze the Colonel.

"Well," he said, "if it can be beaten, I'll beat it."

"It was as if the Irish in him was responding to a challenge," said John Cox. "He was getting ready to fight."

"We had several corroborations," said Ciliberti, "but with a man like the Colonel, you touch every base, and I told him I wanted him to go up to Roswell Park Memorial Institute in Buffalo and let them take a look. He didn't want to, said he had been looked at enough, that he trusted us. He finally did, and the chief at Roswell saw him, and agreed with what we had done here at Jewish, our diagnosis and course of treatment. KFC was very solicitous. Flew him up and back. So was John Y.

"I started trying to protect him more than before. You know, from the start, he was sure he was going to beat it. We knew he wouldn't. Leukemia is often curable in kids, but not with adults, not this kind. We talked about it. He was very co-operative. The big thing on his mind was his ninetieth birthday party. He said to me, 'They've got this big party scheduled for me; do you think I can make it?' And I said, 'Sure. You'll make it to the party.' Although, to tell the truth, I had some real reservations about it."

As Dr. Ciliberti explained, leukemia is a puzzling disease. Leukemias—there are several forms—are cancers of the blood-forming tissues of the body, the bone marrow and lymph nodes. Acute, stem-cell leukemia prompts the bone marrow to produce malignant, primitive white cells which are scattered throughout the bloodstream and lymph and lodge in other blood-forming tissues where they continue to multiply. In acute leukemia, the form from which the Colonel was suffering, leukemic cells may also infiltrate other tissues, and lead to anemia, susceptibility to bleeding, and a tendency to develop severe infections that the body would ordinarily combat with the red blood cells that are now outnumbered. Prior to the development of drugs used in chemotherapy, acute leukemia patients, especially young ones, usually lived only a few weeks. But with chemotherapy, the patient may enjoy remission, during which symptoms are relieved and normal health is temporarily restored.

Some doctors, hoping to encourage hope in the leukemic patient, tend to gloss over the temporary aspect of the improvement, and emphasize the possibility of remission. Many patients read into the doctor's words what they want to hear, and the Colonel may well have fallen into this category. In any event, he returned home full of hope and determination to "fight this thing." But hardly had he begun to fight when he suffered a setback. On the last day of June, he developed a fever, felt weak, and started having difficulty breathing. That afternoon he again entered Jewish Hospital, suffering from what the doctors at once diagnosed as another case of pneumonia.

It was one more in a procession of events whose tempo was quickening. But he responded well to medication, and after three days the doctors were able to continue with his Monday and Wednesday treatments for the blood cancer. He was in the hospital for twelve days this time.

"It seemed like three months," he said as he left, and for the first time he used a motorized wheelchair. "I guess I needed it. The doctors know what they're doing." He added that it was almost worth the trip to the hospital to hear from so many old friends and well-wishers.

The show of concern was impressive. Visitors packed the waiting room and the corridor leading to the Colonel's room, though the doctors insisted that he could see only a few. Gifts, letters, and get-well cards arrived by the thousands. After the first day, the flowers and plants had to be sent either to the Sanders home or to KFC offices. House plants alone filled the entry hall of the Sanders home. A huge chicken fashioned from white chrysanthemums sat on the coffee table. A friend from Georgia sent a bushel of sweet white onions, another in South Africa sent a $200 arrangement of flowers and fruit.

The Colonel was quiet and subdued on his drive home, but later, after he had changed into pajamas, taken a brief nap, and snacked on Bing cherries, he came into the living room to talk to friends and reporters, and he showed no reluctance in talking about his leukemia.

"I think I'm getting along pretty well," he said. "You don't expect a fellow to look better than me at this age, anyway." He reported, with obvious pride, that he had gotten letters and cards from every country in the world. "Well, every *civilized* country anyhow." And he refused to be downhearted about his leukemia.

"I never had leukemia before," he said, apropos of nothing. "It's a new racket for me and my doctor. But I'm not scared. No, hell no, not scared. I felt like we could possibly control it. If we don't, why, if I've lived this long, I've lived a good lifetime."

Claudia, too, refused to be gloomy on the subject.

"I don't feel there's any use being scared," she said, relaxing in a large armchair near her husband. "If he doesn't live over it, then that's just one way that you can go." The Colonel nodded agreement. It was good to be home, he said. In the hospital, you couldn't get a decent nap for people coming in all the time to give you medicine, shots, do something to you.

"I didn't rely on that hospital food, either," he said with a smug grin. "Most of the time I ate chicken. No, no, not fried—chicken casserole. My little miss here cooked it," he pointed toward Claudia, who smiled at the praise.

But his stay at home was brief. He came home on July 12. On July 16, he was back in the hospital. He had been having difficulty breathing. The next day he underwent an operation for a congestion that was restricting his esophagus. But once more, he bounced right back.

"It was certainly not pleasant," John Cox announced, "but it was not serious, and the Colonel is feeling fine and should be going home in a couple of days." Sure enough, two days later he went home.

But it was clear that there would be no vacation trip this year. His March of Dimes tour was called off, though he posed for pictures with Missy Jablonski, the March of Dimes "Poster Girl" for the year, and announced that Kentucky Fried Chicken stores were going to make a special effort to raise money for the March since he wasn't going to be able to do much himself. He was now in his wheelchair most of the time.

But as his ninetieth birthday approached, he rallied visibly. And on September 2, his doctors announced that his leukemia was in remission. "Well, I expected it," he said. "But it isn't me," he added quickly. "It's my doctor and the good Lord taking care of this for us. When you got what I've got, it's in their hands, don't you see. In the past few days, I've gotten telegrams and letters and prayers from all over the world. With that kind of caring, I figured that God would be on my side."

To mark his ninetieth milestone, KFC staged a huge, three-day party, built around the Colonel's birthday and featuring a three-day Bluegrass Music Festival. On September 7, two days before his actual birthday, the Colonel moved into a suite atop the Galt House, overlooking Louisville's Riverfront Belvedere, where the actual partying was done. Even in his wheelchair, he enjoyed himself greatly. On the first night of the festival, Phyllis Brown led a crowd of more than ten thousand singing, "Happy birthday, dear Colonel." He insisted on walking out on a balcony overlooking the throng and waving his thanks. The crowd cheered for five minutes. The next morning drew another whistling, singing, and guitar-accompanied ovation when he appeared onstage to light the candle on his eight-foot-tall birthday cake, And he announced that KFC stores had raised $625,000 for the March of Dimes, mostly during the Fourth of July weekend campaign. "I think it would have been more if I hadn't been in the hospital," he said. "Well, next year I won't be."

Photographers, reporters, TV cameramen, and partygoers crowded around him as he tried to leave the stage. Missy Jablonski handed him a piece of cake, and after saying that he was strictly forbidden to eat cake, he ate it. He tried to lift Missy into his lap, but couldn't. "My goodness, you're heavy," he said. A TV crew recorded the event for posterity. Children pressed around him. A mother held her child up so she could touch him.

"How do you feel, Colonel?" several reporters asked.

"I feel fine," he said. "Just fine. Being ninety is just a milestone on the way to being one hundred. I've got nine [this was never explained; he meant ten] years to go. I'll just take them one at a time. Then, when I get there, I can have a couple of years as a senior citizen with nothing to do."

The crowd, estimated at thirty-five thousand, gave him a huge cheer as his chair was lifted down and he was whisked into the hotel.

"I think I can survive leukemia," he told a reporter, "but I'm not sure about these parties. They're getting bigger, and I'm getting older."

For two months, the Colonel seemed to be holding his own in the battle to hold off time and the inexorable sickness that was slowly taking its toll of his body. Twice a week, Dick Miller drove him to the doctor's office in Louisville for his cancer treatment. At least once a week, he drove him to KFC headquarters, where he sat in his old office for a few minutes, signed whatever letters or requests for autographs needed to be signed, and occasionally spent some time with people visiting the museum. On Sundays, if he did not feel like going in to the First Christian Church in Shelbyville, he would sometimes listen to Jerry Falwell on television. When he missed church, the Reverend Ed Cayce would usually drop by the house sometime during the day. The two men had known each other since 1939, when Cayce would occasionally eat at Sanders Cafe in Corbin, and they had become close friends since the Colonel moved to Shelbyville.

Cayce's first wife died of cancer in 1962, and it was during that time that the friendship between the two men matured.

"I've never seen anyone so attentive and so tenderhearted," said Cayce. "Those people who think of Harland Sanders as being only the rough, tough man never saw the gentle, loving human underneath."

The Colonel, a year or so later, decided that his minister needed a wife, and appointed himself matchmaker. During his business travels, he had met a Texas businesswoman who, he concluded, just fit the bill, and arranged to ask Cayce over to his house when the woman, Eleanor Arrechea, was in Kentucky on business. Cayce had an idea what was going on, and managed to sidestep the Colonel's trap several times, declining one invitation after another. The Colonel was not about to be so easily put off, and persuaded Mrs. Arrechea to stay over and attend Sunday services at Cayce's church.

"And he was right," said Cayce. "He played Cupid from then until we were married in 1973." The Colonel served as best man.

Now the memories of battles and bruises were fading, and

the good deeds of many years were yielding a long, full harvest, as a steady procession of friends, old business acquaintances, employees, and associates made the pilgrimage to the brick home on Kentucky Highway 53. And on October 23, in a ceremony held at KFC headquarters, Governor Brown awarded the Colonel the governor's medallion, the highest civilian award Kentucky can bestow.

Television lights glared and reporters and well-wishers jammed the museum as the Colonel wheeled into the room. Everyone crowded around, asking him how he felt, telling him he looked great. Then Brown, graying and thirty pounds heavier than when he had persuaded the Colonel to sell Kentucky Fried Chicken, breezed through the crowd and gave the Colonel a hearty hug.

"Mornin', Colonel," he said casually. The Colonel gave him a long, level look.

"Where's Phyllis?" he asked crossly. Brown explained that Phyllis was home, taking care of the Browns' new son, Lincoln George Brown. ("Wonder how many names that kid's going to have by the time they get through naming him?" the Colonel had grumbled to the author a few weeks earlier. "I think they're trying to name him for everybody on both sides of the family and throw in anybody ever run for office. Plus President Lincoln.")

Brown made a brief speech, calling the Colonel "a true legend" who "changed the eating habits of the world," and "a fine example for senior citizens, a man of native intelligence, wisdom, and special imagination, who spread the image of Kentucky with that of Colonel Sanders." He then opened a red-velvet-covered box and handed the Colonel a gold medallion, about four inches in diameter. The Colonel held it up for the photographers and cameramen.

"I so appreciate this medal," he said. The audience burst into applause. "Thank you so much."

Two weeks later, on November 7, the Colonel once more made the trip to Jewish Hospital, this time for what doctors diagnosed as an infection of the kidneys and bladder. From the day he entered the hospital, it was evident to everyone who saw him that he was going to face more than he had weathered before. He seemed grateful to get into bed, lay back with a sigh, and close his eyes. When Governor Brown visited him two days later, and asked, "How's it going, Colonel?" the old man looked at him for a moment, blinked, and breathing heavily, said, "I feel pretty good. Yeah, pretty good."

But he didn't feel pretty good. He responded very slowly to the antibiotics given him for his kidney infection. He seemed to respond only to Claudia. He seemed to perk up a little when she came into the room, and upon waking he would look to see if she was there, nodding slightly if he saw her.

"There was some friction within the family during the last illness," said Dr. Ciliberti. "Nothing said or done, just something you felt. If other members of the family came, Claudia would quietly make herself scarce, go out and get coffee or something. And the Colonel never seemed to care much who else came; at least, no other visitor could make an improvement in him. Claudia was the one loyal member of the family, and he regarded her very highly. She took care of him. But there was no doubt about who ran the show. He gave the orders. Right to the very end.

"A curious thing. I tried to get the Colonel to leave some money to Jewish Hospital, but I couldn't. Because he didn't know what Jewish did for him, and I couldn't tell him. But just a couple of weeks before he died, we got a threatening phone call, someone said he was going to kill the Colonel. A crank call, no doubt, but with a man like the Colonel, you had to take it seriously, and Jewish put guards on his room around the clock. You couldn't get into the room without clearance. It made a lot of trouble, but there was no alternative. I would ask a cardiologist to go see him and he couldn't get in because he hadn't been cleared and he'd call me and say, 'What the hell's going on?' "

On November 14, the Colonel developed pneumonia yet again, and was listed in critical condition. Now the doctors were fighting not to stem infection, but to save his life. The next day his condition worsened and friends and family members were told to expect bad news. But two days later he rallied, sat up, and said he would like visitors.

"Don't write me off yet," he told reporters. "I'm not down yet. I sure ain't out." On November 19, doctors told reporters that they were elated, "can hardly believe it. The man has a will that forces him to live."

But by the next day, he was feeling worse. He had contracted pneumonia still again, was again put into intensive care.

"An interesting thing happened there toward the end," said Dr. Ciliberti. "One time, we thought he was about to die. He was no longer responsive, in a coma. We didn't know exactly why. But, after all, he had leukemia, diabetes, pneumonia, a stroke, arthritis, arterial problems, eye problems, heart trouble; he had a kidney failure, bladder infection, chronic constipation. I figured it was the end, except for one possibility.

"Before we discovered he had leukemia, he had gotten up one night to go to the bathroom and had fallen. We decided he had had a slight seizure, because he became very confused. I put him in the hospital, figured he had had a seizure, like a mild form of epilepsy, which is not unusual as you get older. I gave him some medicine, and he had not had another seizure, though when he came into the hospital this last time, he had not been taking his antiseizure medicine, and with everything else wrong, we had not bothered about it.

"Now he was comatose and I couldn't figure out what was going on, so I said to my interns and students, 'Let's go ahead and treat him as though he had had a seizure.' That's what we did, treated him with the appropriate drugs and within a few hours he was better and everyone was saying it was a miracle. It wasn't, but it gave him another three weeks or so."

For the next twenty days, the Colonel seldom spoke, as though marshalling all of his once-exuberant energy, once-vigorous strength for the battle to live. Improving, declining, as though borne on waves of time, he slipped slowly downhill. On Monday, December 15, he seemed noticeably weaker, and

Claudia remained in his room throughout the day. After he dropped off to sleep that night, she left and was driven home, promising to return the next day. The next morning, Dr. Ciliberti came in shortly after six-thirty to check on him, and found him weak but conscious, and in seemingly good spirits.

"Well, Colonel," he said, "how're you feeling?"

"About the same," the Colonel replied, adding that he had slept well. But he said he didn't want any breakfast, just wanted to rest. Dr. Ciliberti told him he would drop back by in an hour or so.

There was nothing to do but wait. And there was not long to wait. At seven-forty, as daylight was seeping across the land, turning out the street lights and slanting through the windows of the hospital, the nurse checked and found that Colonel Harland David Sanders was dead.

Epilogue

When a man dies who has made an impact on his time and fellow man, those left behind try, as they must, to assess not only his impact but the facets of personality and character that produced that effect. And so, even as the flags flapped at half-mast in the winter wind of Kentucky, and those who had loved Harland Sanders prepared to conduct for him those rites that signal the certainty of end, the hope of beginning, the post-mortems for him were being held.

Most were in glowing tribute. His typically American virtues, or what we like to see as typically American virtues—work, courage, perseverance, and generosity—were cited as reason for and justification of his wealth and success. For Americans have long been dichotomous on the subject of money, idolizing those who make it, yet feeling that having it is somehow evil, and so they seek ways to explain how good men may still get rich, and rich men may still be good, forgetting that the Bible says that it is the love of money, not money itself, that is the root of evil. And so for many it became necessary to depict Harland the brawler as Colonel Sanders the philanthropist, though he was obviously both.

At the same time, there were those who simply did not like the man. That is hardly surprising. It is unlikely that a man of such decided personal traits could have lived ninety years without leaving bruises in his wake. Indeed, he once joked that he was popular only because he had outlived his enemies. Not all of them, of course. Just as there were those who saw him as saint, so were there those who considered him a coarse, self-centered boor, loving only those he needed, generous with those who adored him.

There is truth in both assessments. There is no doubt that Harland Sanders had a "vile tongue and violent temper," though both lost some of their jagged edges to time and the gentling chemistry of experience. Some called him a hypocrite for flowering the air with Biblical quotations one moment, turning it blue with profanity the next. His parental prudery was in strange contrast to his personal lechery, or so they decided. His generosity was at odds with his appetite for violence.

But there is no evidence that he was more lecherous than the average man. It is a measure of him, perhaps, that he cursed himself for cursing, in a day when profanity had become common. It is possible that he was sincere when he insisted that he fought only against injustice. It was at least an excuse, and possibly one that he could accept for what was in reality nothing more than a bad temper.

He was a creature of contradictions, as are most men. He was the penny-pinching philanthropist who could give away a company but hated to pick up a check. He was self-conscious about his lack of urbanity, yet affected "hick" grammar that made him more the redneck than he was. He was vain about his appearance and attire, embarrassed by his lack of education. He made mistakes, and often blamed them on others (as he blamed John Brown for a contract to which he agreed). Yet in all his suffering, he would not complain. He never whined.

It is important to remember that he was a superb, instinctive actor, with an actor's love of the grand gesture, the calculated impression. He could hurl a knife at the cook in fury, then five seconds later walk through the door, bow, smile, and charm the customers. Even when standing on tiptoe in financial quicksand, he had to drive a white Cadillac and vacation in Florida, when only the rich vacationed in Florida. He liked to make big entrances, make an impression, attract attention, which he sometimes mistook for respect. It is possible that his temper, his grammar, his profanity—all were staged, to an extent, to shape an image.

Harland Sanders did not question, but believed, and agonized when what he saw as weakness led him astray from those beliefs. He was a man who could not speak easily of love, and who saw tears as weakness. Yet he loved without reservation, and the tenderness it bred showed itself in tears aplenty.

Above all, he was a man of indomitable courage. If we seek the genius of Harland Sanders, we will find it in the fact that he would not be conquered. No matter how often or how brutally life knocked him down, he rose to his feet once more, staggering and bloody perhaps, but determined to stand and try once more. He was unusual in that he would not recognize defeat. He succeeded mainly because he refused to fail.

He was Harland, and the Colonel, and the two were not the same, and it is a mistake to assess the one and not the other, as some have tried to do. The kind and gracious Colonel had his roots in the tough, fiery, persevering Harland. Harland's hardness became the Colonel's endurance. In the final analysis, he must be considered as the sum of his roles, for his story is that of all of them—the boy, Harland, the Colonel. A man. A life.